WORDS AT THE WEDDING

WORDS AT THE WEDDING

Reflections on Making and Keeping
"The Promise"

William J. Byron, SJ

Paulist Press
New York/Mahwah, NJ

Cover photograph of wedding, far left, courtesy of Drew and Paula Brown

Cover design by Sharyn Banks
Book design by Lynn Else

Library of Congress Cataloging-in-Publication Data

Byron William J., 1927–
    Words at the wedding : reflections on making and keeping "the promise" / William J. Byron.
        p. cm.
    ISBN 978-0-8091-4403-7 (alk. paper)
    1. Marriage—Religious aspects—Christianity. 2. Weddings. I. Title.
    BV835.B97 2007
    234'.165—dc22

                                                    2006034096

Published by Paulist Press
997 Macarthur Boulevard
Mahwah, New Jersey 07430

www.paulistpress.com

Printed and bound in the
United States of America

Dedicated
to the many couples
whose weddings I've witnessed
over the years

Contents

Appreciations

The Publisher gratefully acknowledges use of the following materials:

Gratitude to Samuel Hazo, Director of the International Poetry Forum in Pittsburgh, Pennsylvania, for permission to include "How Married People Argue" in Chapter 23.

Excerpts from Michael Francis Pennock, *This Is Our Faith*, in Chapter 18 used with permission of Ave Maria Press, all rights reserved.

The song "Wherever You Go" from the album *Wherever You Go*, © 1972 The Benedictine Foundation of the State of Vermont, Inc. Weston Priory, Weston, VT. Used with permission.

Extracts from Boubil and Schönberg's **"LES MISERABLES"** based on the novel by VICTOR HUGO, English lyrics by Herbert Kretzmer. With kind permission of Alain Boubil Music Limited (ASCAP)
Copyright ©1980. Administered by Alain Boubil Music Limited (ASCAP)
All Rights Reserved. International Copyright Secured.
Printed with permission.

Gratitude to Johnny Duhan for use of lyrics from "The Voyage" in Chapter 29 with permission of the composer. Copyright © 1991 John Duhan. All rights reserved.

"The Skin of Our Teeth" © 1927 The Wilder Family LLC. Reprinted by arrangement with The Wilder Family LLC and The Barbara Hogenson Agency, Inc. All rights reserved.

Introduction

This is a book of paragraphs to ponder. It has no long chapters, just a series of reflections of varying length, each capable of prompting personal prayer or shared communication between engaged or married, even longtime married, couples, who have freely chosen to shape their identity in and through the marriage commitment.

The one-word chapter headings are there to emphasize the fact that these are points to ponder before and after the wedding. The pondering will make both wedding ceremony and wedded life more meaningful than anyone at the beginning of the voyage of discovery that is marriage could ever imagine.

This is essentially a book about commitment. Social observers might judge it to be required reading in our age of hesitation about making commitments—a time of cultural erosion of the strength it takes to maintain commitments already made.

As a Catholic priest, I have a point of view about marriage and commitment. That viewpoint has directed my eye over the years to words from literature and life that I've kept in my personal files and employed in wedding homilies. I've used them as well in conversations and marriage-preparation programs with young people. I think of those snippets as "words at the wedding" and offer them here with esteem and affection for the countless couples whose love I've witnessed in the expression of their marriage vows. Some of those brides and grooms are mentioned by name in the chapters that follow. I wish I could have named them all. In any case, all the brides and grooms I've known are in my heart as both they and I grow older and the roots of the love that each of us is called to live run deeper toward the source of all life and love, God our Creator and Lord.

It is my hope that those roots will be watered by the reflections in these pages. May this small book find its way into purses and pockets of those who are engaged, and onto the family bookshelves of married couples who entrusted themselves to God and to each other on the day they made "the promise" that made their marriage.

WJB
Loyola College in Maryland
November 23, 2005

ONE

Sacrifice

Mutual self-sacrifice, not enlightened self-interest, is what makes a marriage work. Ironically, sacrifice becomes the highest form of self-interest in marriage. Without it, the happiness each partner seeks will always remain out of sight and out of reach. Think about that as you consider adopting this opening reflection as a possible "charter" for your marriage.

In the years before the Second Vatican Council (1962–65), the Roman Catholic Church used Latin as its official liturgical language, but English was the language used for an exhortation read in all churches in the United States at the beginning of the wedding ceremony. I've often remarked that the reason for this was the church's fervent hope that the message would be clear and completely understood! It should be noted, as you read what follows, that inclusive language was not common in those days, and "man" was often used to include both man and woman. I've decided not to edit the original text in any way in order to preserve its historical character. I hope no reader will be offended by the absence of inclusive language.

Notice the emergence of the word *sacrifice* in this text. And the important point to remember here is that for a century before the 1960s every bride and groom about to exchange their marriage vows in a Catholic wedding heard the following words:

> *Beloved of Christ. You are about to enter upon a union which is most sacred and most serious. It is most sacred, because established by God Himself. By it, He gave to man a share in the greatest work of creation, the work of the continuation of the human race. And in this way He sanctified human love and enabled man and woman to help each other live as children of God, by sharing a common life under His fatherly care.*
>
> *Because God himself is thus its author, marriage is of its very nature a holy institution, requiring of those who enter into it a complete and unreserved giving of self. But Christ our Lord added to the holiness of marriage an even deeper meaning and a higher beauty. He referred to the love of marriage to describe His own love for His Church, that is, for the people of God whom He redeemed by His own blood. And so He gave to Christians a new vision of what married life ought to be, a life of self-sacrificing love like His own. It is for this reason that His apostle, St. Paul, clearly states that marriage is now and for all time to be considered a great mystery, intimately bound up with the supernatural union of Christ and the Church, which union is also to be its pattern. This union, then, is most serious, because it will bind you together for life in a relationship so close and so intimate, that it will profoundly influence your whole future. That future, with its hopes and dis-*

appointments, its successes and its failures, its pleasures and its pains, its joys and its sorrows, is hidden from your eyes. You know that these elements are mingled in every life, and are to be expected in your own. And so not knowing what is before you, you take each other for better or for worse, for richer or for poorer, in sickness and in health, until death.

Truly, then, these words are most serious. It is a beautiful tribute to your undoubted faith in each other, that recognizing their full import, you are, nevertheless, so willing and ready to pronounce them. And because these words involve such solemn obligations, it is most fitting that you rest the security of your wedded life upon the great principle of self-sacrifice. And so you begin your married life by the voluntary and complete surrender of your individual lives in the interest of that deeper and wider life which you are to have in common. Henceforth you will belong entirely to each other; you will be one in mind, one in heart, and one in affections. And whatever sacrifices you may hereafter be required to make to preserve this mutual life, always make them generously. Sacrifice is usually difficult and irksome. Only love can make it easy, and perfect love can make it a joy. And when love is perfect, the sacrifice is complete. God so loved the world that He gave His only-begotten Son, and the Son so loved us that He gave Himself for our salvation. "Greater love than this no man has, that a man lay down his life for his friends."

No greater blessing can come to your married life than pure conjugal love, loyal and true to the end. May, then, this love with which you join your hands and hearts today never fail, but grow deeper and stronger as the years go on. And if true love and the unselfish spirit of perfect sacrifice guide your every action, you can expect the greatest measure of earthly happiness that may be allotted to man in this vale of tears. The rest is in the hands of God. Nor will God be wanting to your needs; He will pledge you the life-long support of His graces in the holy sacrament which you are now going to receive.

These words can serve as preamble, preface, or presupposition to all that follows in this book. They also stand alone on their own merits to be pondered at any time before, and for many years after, a wedding ceremony. Any faith-committed person or couple can pray and meditate over them at any time before or after making the marriage commitment because they have a timeless quality and profound beauty that reflect the beauty and permanence of marriage.

I read this entire exhortation at the wedding of Frannie Gillin and Mike Cooley at St. Patrick's Church in downtown Philadelphia on August 4, 2001, pointing out that their parents had heard the exact same words many years before. And I quoted the "and so not knowing what is before you" part for Judy Jankowski and Charlie Lyons at their wedding at Holy Trinity in Georgetown on February 10, 2001. I warmly recommend these words to anyone who wants to contemplate or celebrate the deeper meaning of marriage.

TWO
Promise

Words that I like to quote in wedding homilies or talks about permanence of the marriage commitment are taken from Act II of Thornton Wilder's play *The Skin of Our Teeth*. I think I first used them at the wedding of Betty Anne Donnelly and Phil Pulaski in Chatham, Massachusetts on August 24, 1985. I decided to use them again at the wedding of Terri Gillin and Chris Smith in the Villanova University Chapel on October 5, 1985, where they drew an interesting response. After the ceremony, in the bright sunshine outside, Terri's uncle, a veteran of many stage, screen, and television performances, who had flown in from Los Angeles for the wedding, came up to me with a smile and said, "My name's Iggy Wolfington; I'm an actor too!" Apparently, the lines rehearsed in Chatham had gone over well on Philadelphia's Main Line!

In the middle of Act II of Wilder's play, all is not going well in the marriage of Maggie and George Antrobus. He has just told her: "I'm going to marry Miss Fairweather. I shall provide generously for you and the children. In a few years you'll be able to see that it's all for the best. That's all I have to say." Then he adds: "You're a fine woman, Maggie, but—but a man has his own life to lead in the world." And she replies: "Well, after living with you for five thousand years, I guess I have a right to a word or two, haven't I?" Then comes the part I've often quoted in wedding homilies:

Mrs. Antrobus: (calmly, almost dreamily)
I didn't marry you because you were perfect,
   George.
I didn't even marry you because I loved you.
   I married you
because you gave me a promise.
That promise made up for all your faults.
   And the promise
I gave you made up for all of mine. Two
   imperfect people got married
and it was the promise that made the marriage.

Antrobus:
Maggie, I was only nineteen.

Mrs. Antrobus:
And when our children were growing up, it wasn't
   a house
that protected them; and it wasn't our love that
   protected them—
it was that promise.
And when that promise is broken—this can
   happen.

In one of his short stories, "The Music School," John Updike writes: "We are all pilgrims faltering toward divorce." I don't think so. I think we are all humans struggling to keep our promises, and, with the help of God, all of us can and most of us will.

In the Stephen Vincent Benet short story "Everybody Was Very Nice," a divorced and remarried narrator, speaking of the divorces and remarriages of college classmates and others in his suburban community, asks a happily married friend for his "recipe for a happy marriage." Acknowledging in reply that he and his wife Nan were, perhaps, "exceptions," the still-married friend says:

> [T]here comes a time, no matter what the intention, when a new face heaves into view and a spark lights. I'm no Adonis, God knows, but it's happened to me once or twice. And I know what I do then. I run. I run like a rabbit. It isn't courageous or adventurous or fine. It isn't even particularly moral, as I think about morals. But I run. Because, when all's said and done, it takes two people to make a love affair and you can't have it when one's not there. And, dammit, Nan knows it, that's the trouble. She'd ask Helen of Troy to dinner just to see me run.

Recipes from both literature and life all point to the promise as the central ingredient of a happy marriage. Make it, keep it, run when you have to, but walk the promise hand in hand, joined at the heart, and trusting in God, whose pledge you have for "lifelong support" every inch of the way.

THREE

Presence

My niece Martamarie Byron married David Geilfuss around the time that public television brought Ken Burns's famous documentary on the Civil War into homes all across America. Viewing that program, I was struck by a letter the narrator read from a young husband to his wife. It was written by Major Sullivan Ballou, a Union officer in the Second Rhode Island Regiment, to his young wife Sarah on July 14, 1861. Just a few days later, Sullivan Ballou died during the first battle of Bull Run.

Instead of working words from that beautiful letter into the wedding homily, I transcribed it from the sound track and gave the text to Martamarie and David to be read aloud to one another from time to time throughout their years together. In a cover letter I wrote on their wedding day, I said: "The enclosure is something I want you to have and to share. It is poetic and poignant, sad and exquisitely beautiful. You probably heard these words as you watched the Ken Burns television documentary on the Civil War two or three weeks ago. They are words not about war or death, but about love—the kind of love that I hope will be yours in the marriage built on the promises you made to one another today."

My dear Sarah, the indications are very strong that we will move in a few days, perhaps tomorrow. Lest I should not be able to write again, I feel impelled to write a few lines that may fall into your eye when I shall be no more....

Sarah, my love for you is deathless. It seems to bind me with mighty cables that nothing but omnipotence can break, and yet my love of country comes over me like a strong wind and airs me irresistibly on with all these chains to the battlefield. The memory of the blissful moments I have spent with you comes creeping over me, and I feel most gratified to God and to you that I have enjoyed them so long, and hard it is for me to give them up and burn to ashes the hopes of future years when, God willing, we might have lived and loved together and seen our sons grow up to honorable manhood around us.

I have, I know, but few and small claims upon divine providence, but something whispers to me. Perhaps it is the wafted prayer of my little Edgar that I shall return to my loved ones unharmed. If I do not, dear Sarah, never forget how much I love you, and when my last breath escapes me on the battlefield, it will whisper your name.

Forgive me my many faults and the many pains I've caused you, how thoughtless and foolish I have oftentimes been, how gladly I would wash out with my tears every little spot upon your happiness.

But oh, Sarah, if the dead can come back to this earth and flit unseen around those they loved, I shall always be near you in the gladdest days and in the darkest nights always, always, and if there be a soft breeze upon your cheek, this shall be my breath as the cool air fans your throbbing temple. It shall be my spirit passing by.

Sarah, do not mourn me dead. Think I am gone, and wait for me, for we shall meet again.

FOUR

Commitment

The erosion of commitment in modern marriage is the only basis for finding any humor at all in a *New Yorker* cartoon that shows a matronly lady asking a young engaged couple, "Are you planning a long marriage after the ceremony?"

When I officiated at the wedding of Jimmy O'Reilly and Cheri Hoskins at Port Henry, New York, on Lake Champlain in the late 1980s, I spoke about commitment and borrowed from a book that I had just finished reading a few days before the wedding. The title of the book is *The Postponed Generation*. The author is Susan Littwin, who, I assured Cheri and Jim, was not writing about them specifically, since she did not know them. She was, however, writing about their generation.

> One senses that gifted young adults want what their parents have and more. They want personal gratification as part of the career bargain. They would like to achieve and have influence and recognition, but they are unwilling to take the risk. They talk a lot about freedom and adventure, which often turn out to be code words for not making a commitment. For as long as they haven't made a commitment, their illusions about life

*remain unchallenged. Caught between their sense
of entitlement and their fear of failure, they live in
a fantasy land of infinite choices.* (p. 64)

This writer notes, "there is, in fact, a wedding boom.
But there is no marriage boom." And the point she is making, of course, is that it takes more than a wedding ceremony
to make a marriage; it takes commitment.

What is happening is that we are shifting undeniably and inexorably from a family-oriented society to a society of individuals. (p. 218)

*But today's young adults aren't just victims of
social change. Their personality as a generation
makes them very much part of the change.
Commitment to a relationship is just as difficult
for them as commitment to a career or a point of
view. It is one more act that might define them and
therefore limit their potential.* (p. 219)

What "The Postponed Generation" is postponing, says
Susan Littwin, is commitment.

When the wedding bells ring, they are sounding a call to
commitment. On their wedding day, a man and a woman
define themselves as husband and wife; they are no longer two,
but one. They happily agree to limit their potential for other
choices, for other persons and places. They choose each other,
and in the choice they willingly exclude all the alternatives.

Our cultural hesitation to make that kind of commitment leads curiously, unwittingly, even tragically, to the postponement of fundamental happiness.

A selection from the Gospel of St. John, often read at weddings, highlights the words of Jesus about committed love, self-sacrificing love. And in that passage from Scripture (John 15:9–17), Jesus says, "I have said these things to you so that my joy may be in you, and that your joy may be complete." He then goes on to lay out his understanding of love: "No one has greater love than this, to lay down one's life for one's friends."

This truth is part of the exhortation quoted in the opening chapter of this book, the words young couples heard over many generations when they came to the altar to pronounce their marriage vows:

> *It is most fitting that you rest the security of your wedded life upon the great principle of self-sacrifice....Sacrifice is usually difficult and irksome. Only love can make it easy, and perfect love can make it a joy.*

The idea of sacrifice is not a congenial one today; it is, in fact, a countercultural Christian challenge to the contemporary world. Through Christian marriage, a compelling witness can be offered to the world to demonstrate that love involves sacrifice, and sacrifice is identified with love. The ultimate key to happiness lies in one's willingness to make that identification a defining characteristic of one's life. Marriage requires this identification and offers in return a joy beyond imagining.

I recall making some of these same points at the wedding of Connie Drobile and Paul Korz in Wayne, Pennsylvania in the summer of 1989. On commitment, I said to them:

> *To make a serious commitment to another person, or to a cause, or both, demands a price. The commitment required for marriage and family is costly, and the fact that you stand ready to pay the price is a sign of your generosity, because the price is unmanageably high only for those whose selfishness is unconscionably deep. But the price is well worth paying; it is the only way to happiness.*

And I might have added a phrase I later found in notes from T. S. Eliot, who spoke of love as "complete complicity costing not less than everything."

FIVE

Forgiveness

It is more than helpful from time to time simply to ponder in quiet prayer the depths of a few of the beautiful passages from Scripture that find their way into the wedding celebration. Here's one from the Letter to the Colossians:

> *As God's chosen ones, holy and beloved, clothe yourselves with compassion, kindness, humility, meekness, and patience. Bear with one another and, if anyone has a complaint against another, forgive each other; just as the Lord has forgiven you, so you also must forgive.*
>
> *Above all, clothe yourselves with love, which binds everything together in perfect harmony. And let the peace of Christ rule in your hearts, to which indeed you were called in the one body. And be thankful.* (3:12–15)

This text emerged in separate contexts, several years apart, in a way that touched profoundly the lives of two couples—one whose marriage had reached the breaking point, the other whose marriage had just begun. Let me explain.

It was a bit of a risk, I knew, to inject a sad, although beautiful, story into the homily I gave at Holy Trinity in

Georgetown, my last wedding as pastor there, in the summer of 2003. The bride and groom, Trisha Morrow and Matt Madden, had selected this passage from Colossians as the second reading for their wedding liturgy. Shortly before their wedding date, I received a letter that reminded me that I had preached on that text from Colossians at a Sunday mass several years before. I took the risk of quoting from this moving and quite personal communication in my words to Matt and Trish.

The letter was from a woman I do not know, a parishioner who wrote to wish me well as I was leaving Holy Trinity and to tell me a story of how, without knowing it, I had touched her life. She explained that she and her husband were married at Trinity in 1974. "Like most long unions," she wrote, "we encountered a rocky period in our marriage, leading to a separation in July of 2000. In December of 2000, on New Year's Eve, he approached me about reconciliation."

She said she reacted to that proposal with "pain and anger," but "I was also very undecided." Her letter went on to say that on the next Sunday, "I attended mass where you gave a sermon on forgiveness. You gave me much to think about." Shortly thereafter, she said, she began meeting with her husband to begin "talking and exploring our mistakes.... Forgiveness is not an easy, instant accomplishment, and I owe you a great appreciation for opening my eyes to that."

Her letter went on to relate that "in the summer of 2002, we traveled to Ireland to celebrate my fiftieth birthday. Unbeknownst to me, he had arranged with the parish priest for us to renew our vows at the Catholic church in Kinsdale, County Cork. It became the highlight of our trip and an opportunity for us to renew our devotion to each other with Christ's blessing."

The writer added that two months later her husband died in a cycling accident. "Although our reconciliation was short, I am indebted to you for teaching me the importance of forgiveness and love in my life."

As I mentioned, Trish and Matt had selected Colossians 3:12–17 for their second reading: "As God's chosen ones, holy and beloved, clothe yourselves with compassion, kindness, humility, meekness, and patience. Bear with one another and, if anyone has a complaint against another, forgive each other; just as the Lord has forgiven you, so you also must forgive."

When I realized that this reading was the one my correspondent heard on the Holy Family Sunday she referenced in her letter, I decided to share the story with Matt and Trish and their wedding guests. In my words at the wedding, I reminded Matt and Trish that love and forgiveness are one. The Letter to the Colossians lists love's central elements. It explains the meaning of love in terms that constitute a charter for a happy marriage. I held in my hand a copy of that Holy Family Sunday homily of three years before, and from it I read my own words:

> *Aware of having been forgiven and yet still needing forgiveness in Jesus Christ, believers should extend to each other forgiveness now and the promise of future forgiveness. That, of course, is*

what it means to forgive as the Lord has forgiven you.

To that I added St. Paul's instruction:

Above all, clothe yourselves with love, which binds everything together in perfect harmony. And let the peace of Christ rule in your hearts, to which indeed you were called in the one body. And be thankful.

These are potent words for newlyweds, never-weds, and those who are hopeful of staying wed when a "rocky period" threatens their marriage.

I write a biweekly syndicated column called "Looking Around" for Catholic News Service. It is a general interest column that allows me a wide enough range of topics to include occasional thoughts about marriage and the family. So I wrote a column about the story I've just related here; it appeared in many papers around the country under the title "When a Rocky Period Threatens a Marriage." To my surprise, it prompted the following letter from Matt Madden:

Trish and I recently received a copy of your September 19th column that ran in The [Boston] Pilot, *in which you reference the homily you delivered at our wedding in July. We appreciated your thoughtful words on love and forgiveness at our wedding and are very happy you were able to share this message with a wider audience.*

We are glad you took "a bit of a risk" to tell a story that demonstrated the importance of for-

giveness in marriage. The words you spoke, as well as those in the Holy Family Sunday Homily you gave us afterward, will certainly be an important part of our lives together as we work to deepen our vocation to celebrate and bear witness to Christ's love as a couple.

What you may not have known is what a particular blessing this "risk" was at our ceremony. Trish's parents, only a year and a half before our wedding, had separated and moved apart. Their struggles as a couple were difficult for them as well as for Trish and me. For a year and a half they took slow but deliberate steps toward reconciliation and forgiveness. Just a few months before our wedding, they resumed living under the same roof to continue their process of reuniting and resuming their lives together. Their progress continues and it is wonderful to witness this power of forgiveness that you spoke of in your homily.

I believe that our wedding preparations were an important part of Mr. and Mrs. Morrow's reconciliation as much as watching their work towards forgiveness was an important part of our spiritual preparation for marriage. Issues of reconciliation, forgiveness, marital strife, and what it means to be a Christian couple pervaded many of my conversations with Trish as we prepared for our wedding. Therefore, it was a special blessing that you chose this theme for your homily on our wedding day....

Thank you for being an important part of our important day. You couldn't have chosen a better message to guide Trish and me, as well as our friends and family, on the day of our wedding. It was a special gift of the Holy Spirit that you were called to take this "risk" at our wedding and a gift for which we are extremely grateful.

Nice to be reminded from time to time about the power of forgiveness!

SIX

Destiny

You are what your deep, driving desire is;
As your desire is, so is your will;
As your will is, so is your deed;
As your deed is, so is your destiny.

These words, taken from the ancient wisdom of the Upanishads, fit neatly into the wedding picture. It is desire that brings any couple to the altar; they are drawn there by their will to wed. So, one might say to such a couple, "As your wedding is, so is your destiny"—a lifelong commitment to love one another.

I said just that to Michael Frost and Christine Jones, who included in the readings they selected for their ceremony a familiar text from the Book of Genesis and also what may well be the most popular of all Scripture passages read at weddings, the famous words of Paul to the Corinthians that outline the meaning of love. Both texts are offered here for your reflection.

> *Then the LORD God said, "It is not good that the man should be alone; I will make him a helper as his partner."...So the LORD God caused a deep*

sleep to fall upon the man, and he slept; then he took one of his ribs and closed up its place with flesh. And the rib that the LORD God had taken from the man he made into a woman and brought her to the man. Then the man said, "This at last is bone of my bones and flesh of my flesh; this one shall be called Woman, for out of Man this one was taken." Therefore a man leaves his father and his mother and clings to his wife, and they become one flesh.   (Gen 2:18, 21–24)

And I said to Michael, who had been a student of mine in his senior year at Georgetown, that "just as the Lord said to Adam, 'It is not good for you to be alone,' God somehow said to you that it would not be good for you to be alone." And I publicly encouraged Michael to hear God saying to him, "Let me create for you a bride."

Just as the Bible story tells us that God took a rib from the side of Adam—the region of the heart—to create a woman, I suggested to Michael that God had drawn from his heart, from his heart's desire, this woman Christine whom both God and he want to be his bride. She is special, I said. She is your equal, I reminded him, and she will in just a moment or two become your wife. Michael brimmed with joy when I added, "You need never be lonely or alone again."

Christine, as countless brides before her, had asked that these words from 1 Corinthians 13 be part of her wedding ceremony:

And I will show you a still more excellent way. If I speak in the tongues of mortals and of angels, but do not have love, I am a noisy gong or a clanging cymbal. And if I have prophetic powers, and understand all mysteries and all knowledge, and if I have all faith, so as to remove mountains, but do not have love, I am nothing....

Love is patient; love is kind; love is not envious or boastful or arrogant or rude. It does not insist on its own way; it is not irritable or resentful; it does not rejoice in wrongdoing, but rejoices in the truth. It bears all things, believes all things, hopes all things, endures all things.

Love never ends. (1 Cor 12:31; 13:1–8)

In my homily I'm sure I said to Michael and Christine, as I almost always say when these words are read at a wedding, that they should check to see if one of their wedding guests is a calligrapher. If so, that person should be asked to apply his or her talent to this beautiful text and give the result, suitable for framing, to the newlyweds. It could adorn their home and serve as a charter or mission statement for the marriage that has just begun.

SEVEN

Conversation

In 1980, Cabrini College in suburban Philadelphia invited me to speak at an honors convocation on any topic of my choice. I selected as a theme: "Liberal Arts and the Future of Families."

The convocation program began with a piano selection beautifully rendered by Madame Agi Jambor, an elderly artist-in-residence who had lived most of her life in a middle European country—Hungary, if I recall correctly. After playing, she remained in the auditorium to hear what I had to say. At the end of the lecture, she came forward and said, "As you were speaking, I recalled the words my late husband used to propose marriage to me when I was just seventeen: 'Will you have a conversation with me for the rest of your life?'"

Here are some of the thoughts that prompted her to recall the moving and memorable question that helped to lay the foundation for her long and happy marriage.

I suggested in the lecture that colleges and universities across the country were not doing a very good job of preparing the young for marriage. If commitment is the cement of the marriage bond, I said, conversation is the reinforcing rod. The colleges, I suggested, could do a better job in preparing the young for stronger commitments and better conversations.

Not that the colleges had to do it all, but more could be done, I thought, in the classroom, in research, and in extracurricular campus life to assist the young to prepare for marriage. I was not talking about a need for sex education or the "how to" techniques of parenting, communicating, and budgeting both time and money. I had in mind a largely neglected four-year opportunity to use the liberal arts to plant within young minds and hearts the "stuff" of lifelong conversations. Having something to talk about, I believed, was a major contributor to keeping marriages together. This is all the more important in our day of mute at-home tele-viewing when, as one social commentator recently remarked, "Television proves that spouses will look at any-thing rather than at each other."

In the early Middle Ages, the seven liberal arts emerged in two packages—the *trivium* (grammar, dialectic, and rhet-oric) and the *quadrivium* (arithmetic, geometry, astronomy, and music). My modern *trivium*—a "three-pack," I call it—would include (1) the language-based arts, (2) psychology, and (3) communications skills. An appropriate "four-pack," I suggest, would be (1) music, (2) history, (3) theology, and (4) the visual arts. Roll these categories as shopping carts through any college curriculum, and you will be able to remove from the shelves a rich array of courses that would give any serious couple plenty to talk about their whole lives long.

Some would prefer other shopping carts, I know, and that, of course, is fine. The more the meatier for future con-versations.

Learning, like love, is immaterial. It is not necessary for one person to have less learning or love so that another person can have more, as would usually be the case in the sharing of material things. If both learning and love are recognized as mutually reinforcing as well as growth-producing, the importance of shared learning for the successful development of what I like to call the "marriage project" will also be recognized. There are so many great books waiting to be read, shared, and talked about!

Here, as I see them, are several of the major problems confronting young people on their way to marriage in the United States today. First, the false expectations many of them entertain about marriage. Second, the evident inability of contemporary young adults (and their parents as well) to communicate effectively in depth and in any of the languages of interpersonal relationships. Third, some young people question the possibility of a permanent commitment in a world of rapid change. A fourth consideration is the issue of money management.

I think it is fair to say that reinforced by materialistic, even hedonistic, advertising, fiction, films, and popular music, the unreflective young groom fully expects to have a twenty-something mate for his entire wedded life. His bride, subject to the same cultural influences, unconsciously expects a marriage marked by adulation and attention beyond any spouse's power to sustain. "Love in action is a harsh and dreadful thing compared to love in dreams," says Father Zossima in *The Brothers Karamazov*. Dreams are not the stuff of solid marriages. As an antidote to the "dreamworks" dimensions of the popular understanding of love, I like to quote James Thurber, who offered this observation in a 1960 *Life Magazine* essay on marriage and the family:

> *My pet antipathy is the bright detergent voice of the average American singer, male or female, yelling or crooning in cheap yammer songs of the day about "love." Americans are brought up without being able to tell love from sex, lust, Snow White, or Ever After. We think of it as a push-button solution, or instant cure, for discontent and a sure road to happiness, whatever it is. By our sentimental ignorance we encourage marriage as a kind of tranquilizing drug. A lady of 47 who has been married 27 years and has six children knows what love really is and she once described it for me like this: "Love is what you've been through with somebody."*

The point I was trying to make at Cabrini, and in similar settings when I've had the opportunity, is simply this: The "been through" will have gone quite well if the "being through" that begins on the wedding day is seen as a long conversation. That conversation can be fed by good books shared, films and stage productions enjoyed and discussed together, visual art and music jointly appreciated, and the unpredictable response of mind and heart to the treasures of the liberal arts once those treasures are opened up and shared.

EIGHT

Laughter

Kim Williams, a naturalist, writer, and, until her death a decade or so ago, a guest commentator on National Public Radio's *All Things Considered*, wrote a book entitled *Kim Williams' Book of Uncommon Sense: A Practical Guide with Ten Rules for Nearly Everything*. Her "uncommon sense" on staying married was simply this:

> *At 9:00 p.m., say to your spouse, "Hey, did I make you laugh today? Did you make me laugh? Well, now's the time!"*

She may have been unaware that her good advice had solid biblical and theological roots:

> *I will greatly rejoice in the LORD,*
>   *my whole being shall exult in my God;*
> *for he has clothed me with the garments of salvation,*
>   *he has covered me with the robe of righteousness,*
> *as a bridegroom decks himself with a garland,*
>   *and as a bride adorns herself with her jewels.*
>
> (Isa 61:10)

NINE

Treasure

Joe Maguire and Patti Joyce selected three interesting readings for their September 21, 1985 wedding at historic Old St. Joseph's Church near Independence Hall in Philadelphia. I want to highlight those selections here so that readers can pause and ponder. I shall then provide a bit of background information to explain the significance of the reading from the Gospel of Matthew with its reference to the "pearl of great price" and the "treasure hidden in a field."

From the Book of Genesis, chapter 2, verses 18–24 (a more complete text than the version quoted in the "Destiny" chapter earlier in this book):

> *The LORD God said: "It is not good that the man should be alone; I will make him a helper as his partner." So out of the ground the LORD God formed every animal of the field and every bird of the air, and brought them to the man to see what he would call them; and whatever the man called every living creature, that was its name. The man gave names to all cattle, and to the birds of the air, and to every animal of the field; but for the man there was not found a helper as his partner.*

So the LORD God caused a deep sleep to fall upon the man, and he slept; then he took one of his ribs and closed up its place with flesh. And the rib that the LORD God had taken from the man he made into a woman and brought her to the man. Then the man said, "This at last is bone of my bones and flesh of my flesh; this one shall be called Woman, for out of Man this one was taken."

Therefore a man leaves his father and his mother and clings to his wife, and they become one flesh.

Patti and Joe also selected a reading from the Letter to the Colossians, chapter 3, verses 12–17 (once again, the "forgiveness" theme):

As God's chosen ones, holy and beloved, clothe yourselves with compassion, kindness, humility, meekness, and patience. Bear with one another and, if anyone has a complaint against another, forgive each other; just as the Lord has forgiven you, so you also must forgive.

Above all, clothe yourselves with love, which binds everything together in perfect harmony. And let the peace of Christ rule in your hearts, to which indeed you were called in one body. And be thankful. Let the word of Christ dwell in you richly; teach and admonish one another in all wisdom; and with gratitude in your hearts sing psalms, hymns, and spiritual songs to God. And whatever you do, in word or deed, do everything in the name of the Lord Jesus, giving thanks to God the Father through him.

And their Gospel reading was from Matthew, chapter 13, verses 44–46:

> *The kingdom of heaven is like treasure hidden in a field, which someone found and hid; then in his joy he goes and sells all that he has and buys that field.*
>
> *Again, the kingdom of heaven is like a merchant in search of fine pearls; on finding one pearl of great value, he went and sold all that he had and bought it.*

Joe chose that Gospel reading. Patti and Joe collaborated in selecting the several readings, but Joe wanted that passage from Matthew's Gospel. He was thrilled to have found a "treasure," a "pearl of great value," in the person of Patti Joyce. He was more than willing to "sell all that he had," to make a full commitment of himself to "purchase" this cherished prize.

A homilist might look at this very short text and wonder if there is enough there to work with by way of extending the proclamation to reach the hearts and minds of those assembled to hear these words at the wedding. I knew something of Joe's story, and I knew why that text meant so much to him.

In more recent years, I heard a social commentator remark that many hesitant and unmarried young men and women are "walking over the broken glass of their parents' marriages." Joe's parents were divorced. His mother was no longer alive. His father, a high school classmate of mine, chose, for no good reason at all, not to be present for his son's wedding. Joe wanted permanence in marriage. He understood value. He knew he had a prize, a treasure, a pearl in Patti with whom he wanted to forge a permanent bond.

So without specific reference to anything in the Maguire family background, this reading gave us all a chance to reflect for a few moments on lasting values and on the difference between prizing and appraising.

Appraisals, I indicated in the homily, are measured and quite matter of fact. We appraise objects and speak of their dollar value. But *prizing* something is altogether different. What we prize we cherish and hold dear. We don't even think of it in terms of dollars; we value what we prize in a way that can only be expressed in commitment, in the gift of self, in letting go in order to hold dear.

That's the difference between prizing and appraising, between valuing and evaluating, and the difference, of course, is love.

There is more than a little confusion surrounding the notion of love in our day (the next chapter will provide an opportunity to consider that confusion and ponder the deeper reality and lasting beauty of love). For the moment, I want to stay with the notion of value. Success in lifting a bit of the confusion about value in our time augurs well for gaining a bit of clarity with respect to the meaning of love.

We live in a society that would be much better off if it thought less about value as a noun and gave more consideration to value as a verb. We tend to objectify value. Our values tend to become what we own and store, what we can measure. The higher the appraisal, we conclude, the higher the value. Our values tend to be expressed in nouns, in objects apart from ourselves. We permit our values to become our "valuables."

But when you think of value as a verb and find yourself saying, "I value this more than that," you bring yourself to a moment of truth as Joe Maguire did on his wedding day. If, for example, you value your life, you have to face up to the question of what you are doing to care for your health. If you value a friend, you have to look to your role in building that friendship.

It is instructive to listen to yourself say, "I really value this or that," and then reflect on how much time you spend *with* (not just thinking about but "with") this or that—family, spouse, friend, books—whomever or whatever you say you value. The measure of your preoccupations is a measure of your valuing when you think of value as a verb.

So, through the selection of this Gospel story, Joe was telling his family and friends gathered there on his wedding day that he valued Patti. Value for him was then and remains today a verb that means love. Love for Joe was the "letting go," the "giving up," the "dropping everything" and "selling all" for the pearl of great price, for the treasure hidden in a field.

Together, Joe and Patti were able to rewrite that Gospel passage into their own lives. They've discovered that marriage begins with a treasure hidden in a field. They found it, bought it, and went off happily holding on to it. They've come more and more over the years to understand that this is why "a man leaves his father and his mother and clings to his wife, and they become one flesh" (Gen 2:24).

They discovered that their marriage could be compared to a merchant looking for fine pearls. Their symbolic "selling," through their wedding vows, of all they "owned" established their marriage and "purchased" the permanence that protects their treasure to this very day.

There are a lot of men like Joe who, throughout history, have known the thrill of discovery of a treasure, a pearl of great price, in marriage. They can appreciate the wisdom of the old saying, "When Adam was lonely, God didn't create for him ten friends; just one wife."

TEN

Love

The "word" on every wedding day is love. Words from bride to groom and groom to bride are words of love. Words from us to God in prayer, and from God to us in the texts from Scripture, speak of love. Wedding feast toasts or anniversary testimonials raise the heart and hand-held glass to love.

Readings from Scripture focus the attention of wedding guests on the idea of love. Listen, for instance, to what Jesus says to his disciples in the Gospel of John, chapter 15, verses 9–17:

> *As the Father has loved me, so I have loved you; abide in my love. If you keep my commandments, you will abide in my love, just as I have kept my Father's commandments and abide in his love. I have said these things to you so that my joy may be in you, and that your joy may be complete.*
>
> *This is my commandment, that you love one another as I have loved you. No one has greater love than this, to lay down one's life for one's friends. You are my friends, if you do what I command you. I do not call you servants any longer, because the servant does not know what the master is doing; but I have called you friends, because*

I have made known to you everything that I have heard from my Father. You did not choose me but I chose you. And I appointed you to go and bear fruit, fruit that will last, so that the Father will give you whatever you ask him in my name. I am giving you these commands so that you may love one another.

Typically, in wedding homilies where this beautiful passage from Scripture is proclaimed, I point out that the "new commandment"—to love one another "as I have loved you"—given here by Jesus to his disciples on the night before he died, implies the existence of an "old commandment." The old commandment, not surprisingly, is found in the Old Testament, in the Book of Leviticus (19:18) and the Book of Deuteronomy (6:5), and elsewhere.

Jesus, the rabbi, quotes the old commandment early in his public life when asked (Matt 22:36–40) about the "greatest commandment" of the law: He responds: "'You shall love the Lord your God with all your heart, and with all your soul, and with all your mind.' This is the greatest and first commandment. And a second is like it: 'You shall love your neighbor as yourself.' On these two commandments hang all the law and the prophets."

But Jesus the priest, at the first mass begun in the upper room on the night before he died, laid down for his followers a new law and gave them a new commandment. They can no longer be content to love their neighbor as they love themselves. It is no longer sufficient to follow a Golden Rule, to "do unto others as you would have them do unto you."

No, the new commandment requires you to love your neighbor "as I have loved you." And this means a willingness to lay down your life for the other as Christ laid down his life for you.

The old ethic of reciprocity—doing for others as they do for you, returning love if love has first been received—has to yield to an ethic of renunciation, to a readiness for self-sacrifice. The new commandment is a revolutionary call to an altogether new and higher level of human love. Christian marriage is an answer to this call.

Married couples literally lay down their lives in service to one another and to the children their love brings to life. It is not heroic run-into-the-burning-building-and-rescue-the-terrified-child kind of love. It is rather a willingness to lay down one's life day by day in consideration of, and self-sacrificing love for, spouse and children.

Sacrifice is usually difficult and irksome. Only love can make it easy, and perfect love can make it a joy.

I quoted these words to Shelagh Cook and Rick Mosback before they exchanged their marriage vows in Stamford, Connecticut on May 22, 1976. The church, I told them, and have repeated to so many other couples over the years, is an experienced and loving mother who wants every bride and groom to understand the importance of sacrifice for the success of any marriage. Then, as so many Jesuits of my generation have done in attempting to make an important homiletic point, I borrowed generously from Walter J.

Burghardt, SJ, whose words describing love are woven into what I said in my effort to put this point across for Shelagh, Rick, and their admiring families and friends:

> *Love is, first of all, sacrifice. Not tragic sacrifice, not tearful sacrifice. But love is giving without hope of receiving. Love is burying dead who do not answer, and clothing naked who do not thank. Love is unselfishly wishing good to others. It is just the opposite of that all-too-human tendency to be jealous of the joy in another's eyes, of the health in another's body, of fame and honor in another's life, and of prosperity in another's home.*
>
> *True love is down-to-earth love, just as God's love was and is so visibly down to earth by virtue of the Incarnation, the enfleshment, of his Son.*
>
> *In commanding us to love, the Lord is not asking us for anything false or unattainable. He is merely asking that we cooperate with grace and allow what is most human in us to become conscious of itself at last.*

I like to pull up old quotations and excerpts from books long out of print that convey words about love written in and for another generation. I then present them to this generation's soon-to-be-marrieds with the suggestion that they rewrite them in a vocabulary and vernacular they can call their own. Think before you write is my suggestion, and talk with one another to shape your thinking. Try it out with these ideas from Boyd Barrett's 1952 book *Life Begins with Love:*

Love is a young soldier at the front, scared and miserable, who writes a cheerful letter home to his parents. Love is a man who promises to find a job for an unfortunate misfit and keeps his promise. Love is a woman, who, on discovering another woman's shameful secret, does not reveal it. Love is a thrifty housewife who takes the best she has in her icebox to lay before an unwanted guest, and serves him with style on her best table linen. Love is a college boy who learns the deaf alphabet in order to converse with a lonely old lady who cannot hear. Love is the one who gives abundantly and gives gladly when a beggar returns to ask another alms. Love is the person who, instead of recriminating, sees his own shortcomings in another's faults. Love is the grateful soul who remembers his indebtedness and repays it as best he can.

Rewriting that paragraph together, as best you can, out of your own experience and in your own words, is a labor of love that I warmly recommend to any couple preparing for marriage or counting their blessings long after the wedding.

ELEVEN

Revelation

When a man and woman express their love for one another in the form of wedding promises—the words of their marriage vows—they make a disclosure not only of their intentions, but of the very nature of God. They are telling us what God is like.

I was helped to understand this by these moving lines in the finale of *Les Miserables:*

> *Take my hand*
> *And lead me to salvation.*
> *Take my love,*
> *For love is everlasting.*
> *And remember*
> *The truth that once was spoken,*
> *To love another person*
> *Is to see the face of God.*

I was in London for a few days in January of 1986, staying in the Mountbatten Hotel in the West End, just a block or two from the theater district. It was my good luck to be able to purchase a single ticket (balcony seat, partially obstructed view) for a same-day performance of this great musical. It wasn't necessary for me to see the full stage. It was more than enough just to hear the full chorus provide a dramatic mounting for these gem-like lyrics: "Take my hand and lead me to salvation," and "To love another person is to see the face of God." I knew as I heard them for the first time that these would become for me words at somebody's wedding!

I've used them often in wedding homilies and always thanked the newlyweds for the revelation, for the disclosure of what God is like. For if loving another person is "to see the face of God," then for us who see love between two persons, we are seeing the lines that trace out the meaning of divinity. The ancient Christian writer Irenaeus put it this way: "As those who see the light are in the light sharing in brilliance, so those who see God are in God sharing his glory, and that glory gives them life. To see God is to share in life."

John the Divine, as John the Evangelist is sometimes called (meaning that his Gospel and Letters are more mystical and theological than the writings of the other evangelists), is often quoted in wedding liturgies. For example:

> *Beloved, let us love one another, because love is*
>   *from God;*
> *everyone who loves is born of God*
> *and knows God.*
> *Whoever does not love does not know God,*
> *for God is love.*   (1 John 4:7–8)

What bride and groom say to one another is a revelation of the really significant in life, of the truly beautiful.

Their presence is a reminder that "God is love." Their willingness to commit themselves unreservedly to each other is a clear indication of what God is like. Consider, for a moment, this familiar formula that conveys their intentions and their hearts' desire:

> *I [groom] take you, [bride], to be my wife. I promise to be true to you in good times and in bad, in sickness and in health. I will love you and honor you all the days of my life.*

> *I [bride] take you, [groom], to be my husband. I promise to be true to you in good times and in bad, in sickness and in health. I will love you and honor you all the days of my life.*

We who witness this exchange see brimming life, deep joy, and great human potential that is not selfishly enclosed, but ready to be selflessly shared (and this generosity tells us a lot about what God is like). When we hear the pledge of permanence and see them exchanging rings, we know that these are symbols of the total gift of self. In this witness to fidelity we get another glimpse of what God is like.

Not to be overlooked at any wedding is the witness of the wedding guests, of family and friends, men and women whose lives are woven over the years into a fabric of love—sometimes rough, sometimes smooth—a fabric that is tear-stained, blood-stained, torn and mended; a fabric that's been spread for feasts and funerals, a wrapper for worries and, with it all, a beautiful tapestry of peace, forgiveness, achievement, and joy. I sometimes invite bride and groom to look around them on their wedding day and see the full spectrum of the loves and lives that have shaped their wedding moment. In the assembly of their families and friends, bride and groom can see the sacredness and seriousness of human life and love. They need look no further to find divinity itself.

TWELVE

Rings

"With this ring, I thee wed."

"_____, take this ring as a sign of my love and fidelity."

The ring, the wedding band, is indeed a sign of love and fidelity. It symbolizes promises made, vows exchanged. It signifies commitment.

I've often let the following lyrics roll around in my mind just to set the stage for a matrimonial play on words: "Casey would waltz with the strawberry blonde, and the band played on....He married the girl with the strawberry curl, and the band played on."

The edit I like to make is this: "And the bands stayed on!" That symbol of love and fidelity—the ring, the wedding band, the sign of committed togetherness—is there on the third finger of the left hand to tell the world, as one songwriter put it, that "Our love is here to stay."

And yet I know there are many who have a "flaps up, rings off" mentality as they take off, sit back, and relax at the beginning of business trips or other kinds of solo flights when a trusting spouse is left behind.

"And I plight unto thee my troth" are the words that immediately followed the "with this ring I thee wed" declaration in the old Roman Catholic wedding ritual as the groom placed the ring on his bride's finger. (There was no provision in the old ritual, by the way, for the bride to place a ring on her groom's finger!) The etymological link between "troth" and "truth" is easy to establish. And "plight," although today thought of more readily as relating to a dangerous circumstance or fearful stress, was, in a now archaic vocabulary, another word for "pledge." Troth, in the solemn language of the wedding ceremony, means pledged faithfulness. And, of course, a "betrothal" is a promise to marry.

Several prayers are available for use by the celebrant in blessing the rings at a Catholic wedding. One is simply, *"May the Lord bless these rings which you give to each other as the sign of your love and fidelity."* Another asks, *"May these rings be a symbol of true faith they [the bride and groom] have in each other, and always remind them of their love."*

My mother graduated from Trinity College in Washington, D.C. in 1918 and immediately went to Philadelphia to begin writing for a daily newspaper, *The North American,* which long ago went out of business. My father came to Philadelphia a year earlier from Lawrence, Massachusetts to begin the study of medicine at Jefferson Medical College. They met, fell in love, married, and eventually settled in a town near Pittsburgh where he practiced his ear-nose-and-throat specialty. He died in 1928 of an illness that would easily have been cured had the antibiotics that are now available everywhere been available then. At age thirty-three my mother was a widow with two infant sons—one two-and-a-half, the other (me) seven months old.

Growing up, I occasionally heard older relatives and family friends speculate discreetly and quietly, of course, as to whether or not my mother would remarry. She was young and attractive I realize now, although like any young boy I then thought of my mother as, well, old! I have no memory at all of any budding resistance or resentment on my part to the prospect of remarriage for my mother. It was simply an issue that never arose; nor do I have any memory of eligible gentlemen friends on the scene to give that question any viability.

When she died at age eighty four, my brother, two years my senior, showed me a letter she had given him many years before, to be opened after her death. "It is a bright, sunny Sunday afternoon and I feel fine," the letter opened. "I've just turned 70 and I want to jot down a few things here that I'd like you to attend to when I die." She then outlined some details about her funeral and listed some possessions that she wanted to pass on to specific grandchildren. She mentioned her wedding ring and wrote: "That's been on my finger since your father put it there on our wedding day. I want it to stay on when I am buried."

It became beautifully and compellingly clear to me upon reading those words why remarriage had never been an option for my mother. Remarriage is often exactly the right step to take for many widows or widowers; their dying spouses sometimes request that they do just that. But not Polly Langton Byron who taught us all a lot about commitment by making sure her ring went with her to the grave.

"Diamonds are forever," say those who cut and sell them. Diamonds are an important component of what economists might think of as the GWP—the "gross wedding product" associated with booming sales in the wedding industry. Diamond rings have no appeal at all to me; I like the simple wedding bands, but I'm a man who will never marry and have neither the mind nor the heart of a bride. I have pity, I have to admit, for the girl or young woman who dreams of getting "her diamond" and once it is on her finger, turns it like a searchlight toward the envious eyes of her friends.

I know; I just don't understand!

But the point I like to make with brides that I meet in the months of preparation on their way to the altar is summed up nicely in a story about Helen Hayes and Charles MacArthur. I once thought this was just a legend, but later learned from Miss Hayes that it is indeed true.

When they were young and "courting," as the expression went in those days, newsman MacArthur gave to the young woman who was later to become the First Lady of the American Theater, a bag of peanuts. He presented them with a flourish and said, "I wish they were emeralds." Many years later, when he was dying, she went to his bedside one day and he gave her an emerald bracelet, saying, "I wish they were peanuts."

Materialism can kill a marriage. Creative simplicity, rooted in love, can make a marriage last a lifetime. That's what a simple wedding band can quietly tell the world!

THIRTEEN

⚮ife

Marriage is a vocation to the service of life.

God is the "Lord and giver of life," according to the creed that Catholics recite aloud at mass on Sundays. Those who are graced with the vocation of marriage are called to find more of life both for themselves and their spouses, and to partner with each other and the Giver of life in bringing new life into the world.

So I am amused when I see the ubiquitous newspaper advertisement, "Sex for Life!" Certainly sex is for life. Sex enables spouses to have life more abundantly, enjoy it more fully, and bring new life into being. But that is not what the newspaper ad is selling. It makes a pitch for the possibility of unending sexual activity suggested by the smiling couple coming up from under the sheets, whose picture appears along with a 1-800 phone number that readers of the ad can use to learn more about endless potency—sex for life!

The *Washington Post* is one of the many newspapers across the country that has been running the "Sex for Life!" advertisement two or three times a week for the past few years. I doubt that anyone at the *Post* gave a moment's reflection to the common ground between the mindset behind those ads and the mentality behind a news story that ran in that newspaper on December 6, 2003 under a headline: "Sexual Revolution Sweeps China's Urban Youth." The article is about a 25-year-old Chinese female journalist, Li Li, whose story "is an emblem of the sexual revolution roaring through China's cities, and it underscores the radical changes in Chinese society and mores over the past ten years."

Li Li's diary, posted on a public web site, gives "a day-to-day account of her feelings and copious sexual activity," making her "an underground hero to China's young." In an interview Li Li said, "Lots of people in my generation are having one-night stands all the time....I live a very contented life. In addition to my work I have a particular hobby—making love—and for making love I have lots of choices, lots of opportunity to change, those resources are endless. I don't need to be responsible for my lovers, and I don't need to get emotionally involved. It's like a CD: if you want to listen, you listen, if you don't, turn it off."

Victor Yuan, who runs China's leading polling agency, cites this young woman as a prominent example of "an aggressive search for individualism and personal liberation occurring among China's young." He then goes on to offer four short sentences that sum up the radical new approach to love and sex by China's youth: "If you have sex, you aren't necessarily in love. If you are in love, you aren't necessarily married. If you are married, you don't necessarily have kids. If you have kids, you don't need to be married."

There are clear echoes in China today of the sexual revolution in the West in the 1960s. It was in that context that syndicated columnist Mark Shields remarked a couple of decades later on American television, "During the sexual revolution, I was a conscientious objector." That is not an option that Li Li finds appealing. "I want freedom," she told the *Washington Post*. "I don't care about your morality. I have the right to make love and the right to enjoy it. I like short relationships. That's just the way I am. I see what I am doing as being pure."

Marriage is a vocation to the service of life. Sex, of course, has a lot to do with both marriage and life—the life of each spouse in their committed relationship, and the new life their married love can bring forth. To view sex as a plaything between a playboy and playmate in a one-night stand is to evacuate not just the beauty, but all meaning as well from the sexual relationship. Sex without reverence and respect for life has no meaning. And a search for meaning in uncommitted sex is a purposeless trip that mistakes pleasure for happiness on the road to nowhere.

What the world—East and West—needs now are many more conscientious objectors to the cultural drift that is pulling sex apart from life, to the tragic detriment of both. Those interested enough to care about this cultural drift will profit from pondering the implications for themselves of this reflection on "The Human Condition" found in Edward Chambers's 2003 book *Roots for Radicals* (Continuum):

> *With every birth, a new source of creativity comes into the world. While all human beings have something in common, no two of us are alike. As finite creatures, our existence is time-limited, and*

so we die. The interplay of creativity, diversity, and limits underlies the struggles, successes, and failures of human existence. All human action and growth—in our families, careers, and community involvements—take place within this existential triad: natality, plurality, and mortality. (p. 55)

Sex does indeed have everything to do with life, and the happy life requires a conscious respect for natality, plurality, and mortality.

FOURTEEN

Faith

"With faith in you and in each other, they pledge their love today."

These words are favorites of mine. They come from the prayer that is often used as the celebrant addresses God at the opening of the Catholic wedding ceremony:

> *Father, you have made the bond of marriage*
> *a holy mystery,*
> *a symbol of Christ's love for his Church.*
> *Hear our prayers for _____ and _____.*
> *With faith in you and in each other*
> *they pledge their love today.*
> *May their lives always bear witness to the reality*
> *of that love.*

Powerful words.

Mark Poggio was a United States Marine when he married Carol Stack on September 14, 1996. I recall getting a bit of mileage out of the Marine motto "Semper Fidelis" in my words at that wedding: "Fidelity is a God-like quality. Whenever you see fidelity or experience faithfulness, you experience God; you learn what God is like—ever faithful. If God is God," I said, "he cannot be anything but faithful to his promises. And you today, Carol and Mark, are committing yourselves to fidelity—Semper Fidelis!"

"Be careful what you pray for," is wise advice to anyone addressing God. To ask that lives lived together in the bond of marriage will "bear witness" to the reality of Christian love is asking a lot of any couple because Christian love requires sacrifice. We know, however, from the opening reflection in this book, that although sacrifice is "usually difficult and irksome,...love can make it easy, and perfect love can make it a joy."

So it is a joyful moment for all assembled there at the wedding ceremony to consider the faith that two young lovers have in God and in each other, the faith that has brought them both to the altar. The words of the prayer I've just quoted sometimes bring the opening tear to admiring eyes from the pews on a given wedding day!

Some couples like to follow this prayer with a reading from the Song of Songs (Song of Solomon), words of the bridegroom to his bride found in chapter 8, verses 6 and 7. Groom to bride or bride to groom, the message is the same. And although the word *faith* does not appear here, it is only faith that makes it possible for one human to say to another:

> *Set me as a seal upon your heart,*
>   *as a seal upon your arm;*
> *for love is strong as death,*
>   *passion fierce as the grave.*
> *Its flashes are flashes of fire,*
>   *a raging flame.*

Many waters cannot quench love,
  neither can floods drown it.
If one offered for love all the wealth of his house,
  it would be utterly scorned.

Faith is the act by which we entrust ourselves to God. Faith is something like a bed of embers waiting to be fanned by reflection and prayer so that the flame of faith-awareness can rise to consciousness. This happens during the months of marriage preparation time and, of course, occurs during the wedding ceremony. Through subsequent years of periodic reflection on their promise and the sacramental grace that sealed it on their wedding day, married couples can deepen their faith in one another and in the God whose providence brought them together in marriage.

The faith-in-God-and-in-each-other challenge is captured in another prayer, this one composed by Teilhard de Chardin, that I like to repeat in wedding ceremonies:

Jesus, Savior of human activity to which you have given meaning, Savior of human suffering to which you have given value, be also the Savior of human unity; compel us to discard our pettiness, and to venture forth, resting upon You, into the uncharted ocean of love.

That, I think, is the kind of faith that only a married couple can know.

Ocean City, New Jersey was part of Jeannine Quain's life from the days of her earliest summers. So when she and

Peter Norris married on September 24, 1994, it was no surprise to family and friends that their wedding took place by the sea, at Our Lady of Good Counsel Church in Ocean City. September is a beautiful month on the Jersey Shore. There were no complaints from any of the guests who had to travel from Philadelphia or beyond to celebrate with Jeannine and Peter on a beautiful September day.

In venturing forth that day "into the uncharted ocean of love," this couple had the sight and sound of the ocean to help them reflect on God's power, God's faithfulness, and God's expansive, boundless love. They knew by faith that all of this was theirs as they moved from that day forward into their promised future.

FIFTEEN

Trust

There is something in the following words of John Henry Cardinal Newman that touch the heart in virtually every stage of a human life. I offer them here for pondering by those preparing for, or looking back on the promise that forged their marriage.

> *I am created to do something or to be something for which no one else is created; I have a place in God's counsels, in God's world, which no one else has; whether I be rich or poor, despised or esteemed by man, God knows me and calls me by name.*
>
> *God has created me to do Him some definite service; He has committed some work to me which He has not committed to another. I have my mission. I may never know it in this life but I shall be told it in the next. Somehow I am necessary for His purposes....*
>
> *I am a link in a chain, a bond of connection between persons. He has not created me for nothing. I shall do good; I shall do His work. I shall be an angel of peace, a preacher of truth in my own place, while not intending it, if I do but keep His commandments.*

Therefore, I will trust Him, whatever, wherever, I am. I can never be thrown away. If I am in sickness, my sickness may serve Him; in perplexity, my perplexity may serve Him; if I am in sorrow, my sorrow may serve Him. He does nothing in vain....He knows what He is about. He may take away my friends, He may throw me among strangers, He may make me feel desolate, make my spirits sink, hide my future from me, still He knows what He is about. (Meditations and Devotions, "Hope in God Creator," March 7, 1848)

Change the "I" to "we," the "my" to "our," and the "me" to "us," and watch your faith in God and in each other begin to deepen as you pray together over the relationship of God's providence to your marriage.

In order to do this, you may first have to attend to a suggestion from Teilhard de Chardin, who once noted with a touch of sadness that humanity is still asleep—"imprisoned in the narrow joys of its little closed loves. A tremendous spiritual power is slumbering in the depths of our multitude, which will manifest itself only when we have learned to break down the barriers of our egoisms." Once those barriers are down, you are ready to trust, ready, in other words, "to venture forth...into the uncharted ocean of love" because the God who called you to this marriage "knows what He is about."

SIXTEEN

Salt

Megan Donnelly and Mike Comeau were married on June 15, 1991 in Chatham, Massachusetts. Matt Gillin and Lisa Connelly were married on May 18, 1996 in Dahlgren Chapel on the campus of Georgetown University in Washington, D.C. I knew both couples well and was not at all surprised when they chose the following selection from the Gospel of Matthew for their respective wedding masses:

You are the salt of the earth;
But if salt has lost its taste, how can its saltiness be
*   restored?*
It is no longer good for anything, but is thrown out
*   and trampled under foot.*
You are the light of the world.
A city built on a hill cannot be hid.
No one after lighting a lamp puts it under the bushel
*   basket,*
*   But on the lampstand, and it gives light to all in*
*   the house.*
In the same way, let your light shine before others,
*   So that they may see your good works*

And give glory to your Father in heaven.
(Matt 5:13–16)

In each of these cases, as in so many others when couples choose the "salt and light" reading, the homilist has two great words that describe the two great people there before him. This text provides an opportunity to inquire into the meaning of salt, the meaning of light, and the meaning, in these two instances, of Megan and Mike, Lisa and Matt.

There are moments when you can see a life turning from what it is, to what it will be. This biblical imagery suggests that the wedding ceremony is, for both bride and groom, a moment of salt and light.

Ordinary table salt enhances the flavor already there in the food to be consumed. Salt is both a seasoning and a preservative. And so is love. And so is man to woman and woman to man in marriage. Each awakens, enlivens, enhances, and energizes the other. Their attraction to one another has matured at the moment of marriage to a commitment grounded in love. But if salt loses its taste (its zing, its savor, its interest), how shall its "saltedness" be restored? It won't be good for anything then but to be tossed out and trodden underfoot. Unless, unless....

Bride and groom have to remember that salt is both seasoning and preservative. Like salt, love can preserve love. Love provides the flavor for a life together. As I told Megan and Mike, "only genuine love is capable of this. And genuine love is fully explained in one word, the most Christian of all words in the Christian vocabulary—sacrifice." And just to underscore the obvious, I went on to say that salt is not the entire meal; something more substantial is involved. And—no surprise!—the something more substantial, the deeper dimension of their love for one another, I pointed out, is sacrifice.

I recall telling Lisa and Matt that in ancient days "salt" was used metaphorically to mean friendship, also to mean intelligence (that's why salt and light go together in this saying of Jesus). To this young couple I said:

> *You are indeed the salt of the earth. You will be salt to one another. You will be faithful friends who, like salt, will preserve and enhance friendship in this world.*
>
> *You are the light of the world—bright and beautiful, lively and intelligent. Let your light be seen by all (no hiding it under a bushel basket). Your lives and light will reflect God's glory. Just as the ancient Christian writer Irenaeus said, "The glory of God is the human person fully alive." As you, Matt and Lisa, become more fully alive to one another through this marriage that begins today, God will be glorified.*

It is wonderful to know that the lively loves of all the Matts and Lisas, Megans and Mikes of the wedded world, will give glory to God so long as love and life endure.

The light metaphor suggests that married love and the love-inspired "good deeds" that issue from that love are not just for the married couple. They have to avoid spinning themselves into a cocoon of disengagement from the needs of others. Through marriage, their capacity to reach out, to see, to help others is doubled, as is their capacity to receive the help and friendship of others in return. This idea is captured in the petitions contained in an optional "Final Blessing" that may be used in the Catholic wedding ceremony:

> *May the peace of Christ live always in your hearts*
> *and in your home.*
> *May you have true friends to stand by you, both*
> *in joy and in sorrow.*
> *May you be ready and willing to help and comfort*
> *all who come to you in need.*
> *And may the blessings promised to the compassionate*
> *be yours in abundance.*
>
> *—Amen.*

Salt and light. The world awaits the enhancement and illumination that every wedding ceremony promises to produce.

When a Catholic wedding is set within the liturgy of a nuptial mass, as more often than not is the case, there is a natural supplement to the salt and light imagery. I call it the "bread and wine" of marriage and have explained it to the couple in the wedding homily in these words:

> *Yours is a sacramental marriage set in the context*
> *of another sacrament, the Eucharist. You not only*
> *seal your marriage covenant with a sacramental*
> *promise, you seal it as well with your communion*
> *in the body and blood of Christ. His body was*
> *broken for you; his blood poured out for your*
> *redemption. He invited you, and all who believe in*

him, to remember him in the breaking of the
bread, as we shall do at this altar in just a little
while. He also challenged you to let others know
that you are his disciples by loving one another,
not in a pampered, sentimental, simplistically
romantic way, but he challenged you to love one
another as he loved you, by a willingness to lay
down your lives for one another. This will not be
a sudden, rising-to-the-crisis, heroic, once-and-for-
all sort of thing; it will be patient, enduring, laying
down your life, day by day, for one another, for
the children you bring into the world, and for
those whom God's providence puts within the
range of your compassion and concern. And you
surely don't need me to remind you that you have
compelling models of this kind of love in your parents; so give thanks to God for them today in this
Eucharist.

Christ asked you to remember him as bread
broken and passed around, as a cup poured out
for others. There you have the bread and wine of
Christian marriage. You draw your strength at the
altar of sacrifice; you demonstrate that you are his
disciples by being bread and wine for one
another—bread broken for the nourishment of the
other, a cup poured out in generous concern for
the other with no thought of retaining or recover-
ing the contents for yourself.

Realism requires the admission that it doesn't
always work out this way. But the deeper realism
of your Christian faith affirms that it can work out
exactly in this way—for your happiness, for the
good of the world, and for the glory of God.

For Lisa and Matt, I added another image that was triggered in my mind by the realization that Lisa is a lawyer. The formula for a happy life that I had been outlining in my words at their wedding was, in fact, a formula for a balanced life. That word *balance* made me think of the familiar scales of justice, the trays in balance on a scale that serve to remind lawyers and judges of their responsibility to promote and protect just relationships. (I apologized to Matt, a dot.com entrepreneur, for not being able to think of an unforced way to put the image of a computer chip to similar homiletic advantage!)

The point I made was this: *Think of yourselves as trays in balance on a scale. Think of your marriage as a balance. What is it that might unbalance either or both of you, and your marriage as well? Give some thought to how the trays of your marriage might become unbalanced through unfairness, unkindness, rudeness, selfishness, resentment, infidelity, unforgiveness, a refusal to trust, to hope, to endure whatever comes* (the opposite "weights" of those values St. Paul listed for the Corinthians in the famous reading Matt and Lisa had heard moments before).

> *Married love can be generated only by two people who see and respect each other as equals, who keep the balance in their committed, contractual relationship.*

To all of this, I hope, any fair-minded person, lawyer or not, will be willing to say, "Amen."

SEVENTEEN

Spirituality

Countless volumes have been written about the spirituality of marriage and many more are sure to come. My purpose in this brief chapter is to outline some spiritual principles that can shape a married couple's outlook and influence their choices in living out, day by day, their vocation to marriage.

The opening chapter in this book, intended to be read and reread before and after the wedding ceremony, contains some spiritual principles, some guidelines for a happy life together in marriage. If, as theologian Dorothy Donnelly once said, spirituality is prayer elevated to a lifestyle, praying over the words of that opening chapter can help you to internalize the principles, which in turn will influence your outlook and decisions.

It is important to remember that marriage is a vocation, a call. God has called you to the married state. You've been called by God to live your life in the setting of this marriage, with this spouse, with the children who may come into the world as the result of your married love. God knows you by name, calls you by name, loves you unreservedly, and cannot be anything but faithful to you. Let these truths become part of your spirituality.

God has invited you to build a marriage and in it to become a more fully human person, to assist your spouse in becoming a more fully human person, and with your spouse, to bring children into the world. This is what you are called to be and to do—to be a spouse and, if God wills it, a parent. You are called to do whatever love demands.

Another important principle, mentioned in previous chapters, but worthy of repetition here, is the identity equation that love is sacrifice and sacrifice is love. "Rest the security of your wedded life upon the great principle of self-sacrifice.... Sacrifice is usually difficult and irksome. Only love can make it easy, and perfect love can make it a joy. And when love is perfect, the sacrifice is complete."

Central to this spirituality is the belief that the marriage vocation is a vocation to the service of life, particularly the life of your spouse and the lives of those who might be born of this union. Your spouse is also called to the service of life in marriage—your life and the lives of those born of your mutual love. Clearly then, your vocation requires that you now live no longer for yourself. This truth requires a lot of pondering before and long after the exchange of vows.

It is helpful to think of yourself as being a vocation, not simply as "having" a vocation, but as one who is being called by a loving, leading, guiding God. God does not just call, leave a message in your voice mail, and hang up. God continues to call you through all the ages and stages of your life. You are the vocation and you must be ready always to respond. The need to be responsive is an important reason for continuously opening yourself up to God in prayer.

You are called by God to be and do other things, of course—to be a lawyer, for example, or teacher, computer scientist, nurse, business person, government worker, or any one of a multitude of employment possibilities. And in your occupation (never to be permitted to become an overriding preoccupation!) you are serving God and your fellow humans. But marriage and family come first for you—for both of you!

Finally, I would note that marriage is an expression of biblical justice. This means fidelity to relationships. Think of your relationship to God, to those with whom you share life on this planet, especially those closest to you. And think of your relationship to the earth itself, which you have as a gift from God. You have a responsibility of fidelity in all three directions: to your God, to your fellow humans, and to the creation that surrounds you (and is intended by God to be there to sustain life in the future after you are gone). Biblical justice looks in these three directions. Marriage expresses biblical justice in an obvious and beautiful way, in a relationship of justice (fidelity) with your spouse.

Your ponderings on the ideas that you lift from these pages, your further prayer, reflection, and conversations about marriage, will uncover for you additional elements of a personal spirituality of marriage that you can make your own. It can be as rich and deep as your generous openness to divine grace permits it to become.

EIGHTEEN

Conscience

There are various divisions of theology, as there are in all other areas of intellectual inquiry. There are, for example, the areas of biblical studies, church history, canon law, liturgy, pastoral theology, and what is called "dogmatic" or "systematic" theology. Theology is an exploration that begins and ends with faith, and journeys into the mystery of God. It is the systematic pursuit of the question "What is God like?"

There is another distinct category of theological inquiry called "moral theology," the guidance the church offers to the believer making his or her way through the choices involved in the practice of life.

There is more to moral theology than a list (long or short) of "dos" and "don'ts." It is also much broader in scope than what an *individual* should or should not choose to do. Moral theology has an important *social* dimension that covers broad societal issues and all the great questions of social justice.

It could be argued that marriage falls, to some extent, within all the categories of theology mentioned above. But this chapter's view will be restricted mainly to moral theology at the micro level, to questions of individual conscience and individual families.

Take a moment to think about what are you saying when you remark, "My conscience is bothering me," or, "I've got a guilty conscience." What is conscience? Everyone has one, but what is it and how should it work?

First of all, it is not an emotion (although it may cause me to be emotionally upset), nor is it a feeling (although it can make me feel very good or very bad). Conscience is a judgment. It declares an action or an attitude to be morally "right" or "wrong," sinful or not. To function correctly, conscience must be fully and properly informed. Conscience is a "voice" that delivers a verdict. It is a voice that must be obeyed. Conscience directs you "to do the right thing."

Personal prayer and reflection on Scripture help to shape one's conscience. Reflection on experience and attention to the views of wise and holy persons also help. Catholic moral theology holds that there is a privileged role for the teaching church in the formation of the individual Catholic's conscience. The church also holds, firmly and explicitly, that no one can be forced to violate his or her properly formed conscience. The church, consistent with its commitment to the principle of respect for human dignity, respects the primacy of conscience as well.

The individual decision maker has the responsibility to make principled judgments. Moral choices lead to actions that are consistent with moral principles. Hence the importance of identifying, articulating, and internalizing the right moral principles. With regard to any particular choice, you have to ask: What is operating as the basis for this choice: is it a principle of convenience? compassion? pleasure? selfishness? justice? love?

In the end, it is *your* choice, to be defended by you on the basis of a defensible principle.

Recall for a moment the predicament in which Huckleberry Finn found himself in the fictional but down-to-earth world of rafts, rivers, and runaway slaves. Huck has integrity and authenticity. He is genuinely incorruptible. Recall the fix he found himself in. He was helping Jim, a runaway slave, to gain his freedom. The law said Jim was property; he belonged to Miss Watson. According to the law, Huck was stealing, taking something that didn't belong to him. In befriending a black man and in treating him as an equal, Huck was acting contrary to both law and custom. Huck had been taught that Jim was not his equal. Huck had internalized the dominant public opinion about the institution of slavery—it was not only acceptable but the quite proper way of doing things. But he began to believe that slavery was wrong; he felt stirrings in himself that prompted him to reject a way that he knew deep down to be unjust and immoral. But it wasn't easy. Listen to him agonize:

> *The more I studied about this the more my conscience went to grinding me, and the more wicked and lowdown and ornery I got to feeling....It made me shiver....I was a-trembling, because I'd got to decide, forever, betwixt two things, and I knowed it. I studied a minute, sort of holding my breath, and then says to myself: All right, then, I'll go to hell.*

And that, of course, marked a break for Huck from both law and religion insofar as they supported the institution of slavery, which he, in his heart of hearts, knew to be plain wrong. "It was awful thoughts and awful words," Huck adds, "but they were said. And I let them stay said; and never thought no more about reforming." Better, perhaps, if he had said, "never thought no more about *con*forming" to unjust laws, to inhuman institutions, to unexamined and unfair social conventions.

Mark Twain's wonderful novel is an indictment of a society that accepted slavery as a way of life. Twain puts Huck and Jim together on a raft as sterling examples of integrity, so much more moral than those "proper people" on dry land. Huck offers the reader an example of courage to live life according to principle, in this case a principle of loyalty and fundamental justice. You act on what, in the depth of your being, you judge to be the right principle no matter what the Miss Watsons of the world think of you, no matter how the prevailing public opinion judges you.

Now this is in no way to suggest that law is to be disrespected or disregarded. It is possible, however, to use the law as a substitute for responsible decision-making, and as a shield against growth-producing choice. So, in all of this, *moral* choice is presupposed; this means principled choice based on the right moral principles, and the right moral principles always point to what is good for you. St. Thomas Aquinas offers the reassuring insight that God is offended by us only when we act against our own good. We all need help in coming to an accurate and unbiased knowledge of what is good for us.

With respect to conscience in marriage, conscientious Catholics have to know and carefully consider their church's teaching about family planning and contraception. In 1994, an official *Catechism of the Catholic Church* was published as a "reference text" or compendium of Catholic teaching. An inexpensive paperback edition was published in the United States by Doubleday under its Image Book imprint in 1995.

Summing up the purpose of marriage, the *Catechism* says, "The conjugal community is established upon the covenant and consent of the spouses. Marriage and family are ordered to the good of the spouses, to the procreation and education of children" (#2249). There you have the twin goals or dual purpose of marriage: the good of the spouses and the procreation of children, sometimes referred to as the "unitive and procreative" ends or purpose of marriage. Without in any way intending to be flip or irreverent, some like to say that sex in marriage is "fun with a purpose."

Under the heading of "The Fecundity of Marriage" (#2366–2379) the *Catechism* repeats the teaching of the 1968 papal encyclical *Humanae Vitae,* namely, that "each and every marriage act must remain open to the transmission of life" (#2366; HV 11).

This Is Our Faith by Michael Francis Pennock (Ave Maria Press, rev. ed., 1998) is an unofficial catechism for adults. It asks and answers as follows important questions that concern those preparing themselves for marriage:

What Does the Church Teach About Family Planning?

The Church teaches that a married couple must follow God's plan that each act of sexual intercourse be open to both the sharing of love and the transmission of life. For just and moral reasons, spouses may regulate the spacing of the birth of their children. The physical and psychological health of a spouse, family finances, or the current number of children could be legitimate factors to consider when a couple determines the size and spacing of their family. However, selfishness or greed—for example, not wanting a child because of a desire to attain a certain materialistic lifestyle— would be sinful motives for practicing birth control.

Moral methods of birth regulation include periodic abstinence from sexual relations and natural family planning methods. These are in harmony with objective criteria of morality because they respect normal, natural bodily functions. They respect the bodies of husband and wife and encourage tenderness and authentic communication. Two popular and effective natural methods of birth control are the sympto-thermal method and the ovulation method, also known as the Billings method. The Family Life Bureau of most dioceses sponsors classes to help train couples in these methods. (p. 307)

What Does the Church Teach About Artificial Means of Contraception?

Church teaching holds that artificial means of contraception are contrary to God's will. Artificial birth *control refers to pills or devices (like condoms or diaphragms) that interfere with the conception of a child. The Church also teaches that sterilization— making the reproductive organs unfruitful—is also wrong except when the organs are diseased and threaten the health of the whole body.*

This teaching rests on the Catholic view that marriage is directed to two aims simultaneously: the procreation (and rearing) of children and the mutual love and affection of the couple. Thus sexual relations which are selfishly engaged in by one partner without taking note of the feelings and desires of the other partner are wrong because one of the aims of marriage—mutual love—is destroyed. Likewise church teaching maintains that any artificial means used to frustrate the natural processes of procreation go against the very nature of marriage. Christian marriage is a sacrament, an effective sign of mutual love and openness to life. To rule out either of these purposes unnaturally or selfishly is to frustrate God's intent which is built into the very nature of marriage.

The classic statement of official church teaching in this regard is found in Pope Paul VI's encyclical entitled Humanae Vitae (Of Human Life):

The church calling men back to the observance of the norms of the natural law, as interpreted by constant doctrine, teaches that each and every marriage act must remain open to the transmission of life (11).

In striving to live the ideal, sometimes people fall short. Thus the pope and the bishops encour-

age married couples to frequent the sacraments of reconciliation and the Eucharist to gain strength from the Lord.

Human life and its transmission should be judged from the point of view of our eternal destiny. The state may not usurp the fundamental rights of parents who have the primary duty to procreate and educate children. (p. 308)

(The Pennock book, much shorter and more readable than the official *Catechism*, is useful for Catholics interested in updating themselves on all aspects of their faith—a need not uncommon among young adults preparing for marriage—and for non-Catholic partners who want to have a better understanding of their spouse's beliefs.)

There is no escaping the importance of conscience in marriage or any other area of human life. As persons, we are the sum of our choices. No human can be a moral nomad and remain a fully human being. Moral principles govern moral choices. That's why it is so important to be clear about the principles that govern your moral decision-making. Conscience requires it.

NINETEEN

Rock

"O come, let us sing to the LORD; let us make a joyful noise to the rock of our salvation!" (Ps 95:1)

The Scripture readings selected by Peggy Finnegan and Mike Donnelly for their wedding mass in Chicago on September 21, 1991, required a bit of explanation. That, of course, is the purpose of any homily; it should be an explanation, an extension of the proclamation, an attempt to fit the passages from Scripture into the faith experience of the hearers and then propose the lessons from Scripture as motives, models, or exhortations for future action. But one of their readings—I'll quote it for you now—required a special word of explanation.

> *Not everyone who says to me, "Lord, Lord," will enter the kingdom of heaven, but only the one who does the will of my Father in heaven.... Everyone then who hears these words of mine and acts on them will be like a wise man who built his house on rock. The rain fell, the floods came, and the winds blew and beat on that house, but it did not fall, because it had been founded on rock. And everyone who hears these words of mine and does not act on them will be like a foolish man who*

built his house on sand. The rain fell, the floods came, and the winds blew and beat against that house, and it fell—and great was its fall!

(Matt 7:21–27)

Peggy wanted all her wedding guests to hear about this scriptural "house" built on a solid rock–foundation because she wanted her wedding and the marriage it inaugurated to have its focus on home and family. She and Mike had agreed to get on with the awesome project of making a house a home, a home like the Finnegan home in Chicago or the Donnelly home in Pittsburgh—each a house on a rock of love-based faith, each a home where seven children received the gift of life, and faith, and love for one another. Out of their Catholic family origins, Peggy told me, she and Mike discovered the common ground of their deeper attraction to one another.

At the reception after the wedding mass, Mike's older brother Chris rode a bicycle onto the hotel ballroom floor and, with champagne glass in hand, proposed a toast that suggested that the attraction, from Mike's side at least, was not rooted only in faith and family, but also in the beauty of Pittsburgh's newest television newscaster, Peggy Finnegan. Mike had seen her on the evening news shortly after she came to town. To his pleasant surprise, he spotted her while she was covering a downtown outdoor event one Saturday morning and he was riding by on his eight-speed bike. A quick detour to his office to pick up a business card enabled Mike Donnelly to ride back and trade on his own Irish name and good looks, leaving the contact information in her hand—all to be followed up with appropriate introductions, calls, dates, and the romance that led to the wedding in Chicago.

In the homily at their wedding, I said, *"The foundation of married life for Peggy and Mike is the rock of faith—faith in God, faith in each other; faith in God's love for them, faith in their love for one another. Their marriage—the 'house' they begin to build today—will not rest on the shifting sands of changing emotions or fragile sentimentality. No, theirs will be grounded in Christian love, a love, as St. Paul described it in First Corinthians, that is 'patient, kind, never jealous, never boastful or conceited, never rude or selfish, that does not take offense, is not resentful, is always ready to excuse, to trust, to hope, and to endure whatever comes.' That's love. That's Finnegan family love, Donnelly family love; Christian love for Christian marriage."*

I thanked Peggy for putting before all of us gathered there that day in the Church of the Assumption in Chicago the image of the house on the rock in the context of the meaning of marriage. I've often thought of how helpful it would be for our whole society if more persons would choose to put a focus on family in the search for meaning in life. To focus elsewhere so often misses the point and, sadly, loses the trail in the search for meaning.

Put the focus on self alone and you will find no deep and lasting meaning in your life. Put the focus on career only, on the accumulation of wealth, on celebrity, on gaining the attention of others, on dominating others, and meaning will surely elude your grasp. You can try intimate union or even human service unrelated to family, and the deeper meaning of human existence will continue to elude you. But put the focus on family, and then you will see, unfolding before your eyes, a map of meaning capable of guiding you to the deepest satisfaction and most enduring happiness attainable in the human condition.

Thanks, Peggy; thanks, Mike!

TWENTY
Fidelity

There is no human institution quite like marriage for its potential to reveal poetically, powerfully, and painfully, the beauty of the God-like attribute of fidelity. "If God is God," a wonderful faith-filled woman once told me as she asked me to plan her funeral, "he can't be anything but faithful to his promises." Her point was that she was ready to face death with confidence. My point here is to recall that earth-bound spousal commitments in marriage last "until death." In its duration "until death," the marriage promise and those who keep it tell us a lot about what God is like.

My cousin Alice Scanlan lost her husband John Bateman to death on the same day that the wife of Mike Doyle, the younger brother of a high school classmate of mine, died. Alice and Mike did not know each other then. Friends who knew them both, mindful of the coincidence of painful separation in their respective lives, arranged for them to meet several years later. The meeting led eventually to love and remarriage in Bala-Cynwyd, Pennsylvania on October 18, 1986.

Adoria Brock lost her husband Elmer during the Kennedy years when he came to Washington to take a sub-cabinet post in the administration of the president he had helped elect. Elmer Brock, in his early thirties and the father of five young boys, suffered from a cancer that put him under the care of a young oncologist Emil (Tom) Frei at the National Institutes of Health in Bethesda, Maryland. Tom assisted Elmer medically but could not hold off a death that came all too soon. Many years later, Tom Frei became a widower. Providence put him back in touch with Adoria, who had not remarried and whose sons were grown and on their own. Tom and Adoria decided to find their future together in a marriage that began in Garrett Park, Maryland on May 16, 1987.

It was my privilege to officiate at both these weddings. In each case, I acknowledged that the circumstances were more than a bit extraordinary. I was there as witness to a promise—a promise to live together "in good times and bad, in sickness and in health until death." Alice and Mike, Adoria and Tom had made that promise before—each to a different and dearly loved spouse. And in each instance, the promise was kept "until death." And it was a delight for me to be able to invite the "products," if you will, the sons and daughters of those previous marriages, to witness in their unique way to promises past that were indeed kept in "good times and in bad, in sickness and in health, until death."

In each case, the first marriage took place in the days when the liturgy of the Catholic Church was all in Latin, the days when that beautiful "exhortation" that serves as the opening reflection in this book was read in its entirety to the bride and groom before they pronounced their vows. I, of course, on the occasion of these second marriages, did not pass up the opportunity to quote the lines about sacrifice being "difficult and irksome," its relationship to love, and the importance of letting "the security of your wedded life rest on the great principle of self-sacrifice." At both the Bateman-Doyle and Brock-Frei weddings, with smiling approval from the parents who stood before me as bride and groom, I relayed that message to their respective offspring in the pews behind them. And then I said: "All of us, family and friends alike, can hear at this moment a joyful 'Amen' to that good advice ringing out from heaven from dear ones, now departed, who are not only with the Lord, but with us here as witnesses to the wisdom of love as sacrifice."

I made the same point for the O'Reilly siblings—daughters and sons of Tom and Jean O'Reilly—when their widower father married Patricia Riordan Brestrup, a widow, in the same St. Anthony's Church in Falls Church, Virginia, where we had gathered some years earlier for the funeral of their dear mother, who was a good friend of mine. There were always a smile in Jean's voice and beaming pride in her eyes when she spoke of any of her children. All of them were there in the pews to witness their father's second marriage. I felt the presence of Jean there too, smiling down on all of us and pleased to have "my Nancy," "my Tommy," "my Peggy," "my John," "my Mike," "my Jimmy," and "my Billy" hear the words that helped their mother move through her life and death to the eternal life she longed to share with all of them.

For the believer, "until death" is the final mile marker on the way to an eternal wedding feast.

TWENTY-ONE

Listening

It isn't often that you can find a full-page ad in the *New York Times* that provides good material for a wedding homily. But there it was on Tuesday, March 18, 1980, and I put the tear sheet in my "words at the wedding" file.

Pictured under an eight-column-wide boldface headline that read "WHAT'S THE POINT OF TALKING, YOU DON'T LISTEN TO ME, ANYWAY," are a young married couple, one looking out a window on the left, the other looking out a window on the right. Beneath the picture are these words:

> *It starts out innocently enough.*
>
> *A man tunes in a football game and tunes out his wife's attempts to be heard.*
>
> *A woman gets so wrapped up in her problems she barely listens as her husband talks about his own.*
>
> *And before long, without even realizing how it came about, a deadly silence starts to grow between them.*
>
> *The fact is, listening, like marriage, is a partnership, a shared responsibility between the person speaking and the person listening. And if the listener doesn't show genuine interest and sensitiv-*

ity to what's being said, the speaker will stop talking. And the communication will fail.

Which is why we at Sperry feel it's critical that we all become better listeners. In our homes. And in our businesses.

We've recently set up special listening programs that Sperry personnel worldwide can attend. And what we're discovering is that when people really know how to listen (and believe us, there's a lot to know) they can actually encourage the speakers to share more of their thoughts and feelings, bringing everyone closer together.

Which is of great value to us when we do business.

And perhaps even greater value when we go home.

Sperry, as the ad copy tells the reader, is Sperry Univac computers, Sperry New Holland farm equipment, Sperry Vickers fluid power systems, and guidance and control equipment from Sperry division and Sperry Flight Systems. Sperry Univac is now known as UNISYS, a worldwide information services and solutions company.

I can't say how well the business has been doing since 1980. But the sign-off statement in this advertisement, "We understand how important it is to listen," reinforces the idea that "listening, like marriage, is a partnership." Business historians can tell you how helpful that advice has been to the business; marriage counselors can assure you that it surely had "greater value" for Sperry employees when they went home.

TWENTY-TWO

Cana

This Gospel story is often read in wedding ceremonies.

On the third day there was a wedding in Cana of Galilee, and the mother of Jesus was there. Jesus and his disciples had also been invited to the wedding. When the wine gave out, the mother of Jesus said to him, "They have no wine." And Jesus said to her, "Woman, what concern is that to you and to me? My hour has not yet come." His mother said to the servants, "Do whatever he tells you."

Now standing there were six stone water jars for the Jewish rites of purification, each holding twenty or thirty gallons. Jesus said to them, "Fill the jars with water." And they filled them up to the brim. He said to them, "Now draw some out, and take it to the chief steward." So they took it. When the steward tasted the water that had become wine, and did not know where it came from (though the servants who had drawn the water knew), the steward called the bridegroom and said to him, "Everyone serves the good wine first, and then the inferior wine after the guests have become drunk. But you have kept the good wine until now." Jesus did this, the first of his

signs, in Cana of Galilee, and revealed his glory;
and his disciples believed in him.   (John 2:1–11)

Couples who select this reading know that their wedding is a celebration and their marriage is a feast. Kristin Kane and Jon Wohfert chose this Gospel for their April 3, 1993, wedding at Our Mother of Consolation Church in Chestnut Hill, Pennsylvania; Frank Roche and Hollie Alexander chose it for theirs on a date I can't recall and in a church I don't remember, but I was there. The weddings are linked in my memory due to the fact that I taught Kristin's father Terry and Frank's dad Frank when they were high school boys many years before at the Jesuit-run Scranton Preparatory School. Weddings have a great way of bridging the generations and bringing old friends together.

The wedding is a party, as the Cana narrative suggests. Kristin and Jon caught the spirit of the party with the following words on the cover of the program that enabled their guests to follow the liturgy: "This day I will marry my friend, the one I laugh with, live for, dream with."

The Cana story offers the opportunity to make the homiletic point that marriage is also a project. Mary plays a central but quiet role in the Cana story. She intervenes on behalf of ordinary people, and as a direct result of her intervention, the power of the Lord becomes a striking reality in an otherwise ordinary human event. She shows how a marriage project can get off to a good start.

There's a lesson there in Mary's words for Hollie and Frank, Kristin and Jon, and any other couple starting out in marriage. Mary spelled that lesson out in the words she used to instruct the waiters: "Do whatever he tells you."

Mary did not say, "He is going to tell you exactly what to do." She says, in effect, "No matter how implausible or strange the instruction sounds, be sure to do it." It is as if she were saying, "Now this isn't going to sound right to you; it may not compute. He's going to tell you to draw water when what we know we need is wine. But no matter what he tells you, no matter how strange it sounds, as long as it is the Lord who is speaking, do it. Do whatever he tells you."

These words serve to remind family and friends of the need to pray for the newlyweds, to pray that they will remain open to God's will, attentive to God's word, in order to follow wherever divine inspiration leads, to do whatever God would have them do.

Unless they listen, God will be unable to guide their marriage project. How will they be able to do "whatever he tells them" if they never listen, never give God some quiet time, never pray? Listening to each other will always be important. Even more important will be their success in listening together to the God who called them to their own Cana in their own time.

Any modern Cana couple should be encouraged to see Jesus through Mary's eyes. He is young and smiling, a friend willing to be of assistance to them. If they think of water as a metaphor for grace, they can imagine themselves as two stone jars, waiting to be filled with the grace of this sacrament and thus become fine wine for one another. The quiet miracle is the result of divine power present at their wedding in the person of Jesus. Just as "his disciples began to believe in him" because of the miracle at Cana, any Christian couple can experience a deepening of faith through the miracle of their own marriage bond.

TWENTY-THREE

Argument

The Jesuit theologian John Courtney Murray was fond of quoting a remark made by the British Dominican Thomas Gilby: "Civilizations rest on men locked in argument." "Men" means all of us, of course, and the point of this observation is that reasoned argument is a foundation of civility in daily life. For our purposes here, the saying might just as well read: "Solid marriages rest on men and women locked in respectful argument."

The late speaker of the U.S. House of Representatives, Sam Rayburn, used to say, "When two people always agree about everything, it only proves that one of them is doing all the thinking." Thinking spouses will inevitably disagree. The trick is to disagree agreeably.

In Sylvia Ashton-Warner's book *Teaching* you will find this bit of wisdom:

> *A woman said to me once so proudly, "My family never quarrels." I was young at the time and our children were young and I thought, "How wonderful! If only I could say that." But I'm not young now and I know better. When I look back on that family who never quarreled I remember*

their passivity; the slow eyes that did not flash; on the parents' faces, no grooves that tears had scoured. I know now that it takes passion and energy to make a quarrel...of the magnificent sort. Magnificent rows, magnificent reconciliations; the surging and soaring of magnificent feeling.

A friend of mine who understood the value of argument would often preface a contentious point by saying, "I have to say this now with some feeling." Communication based on feeling can be a deeper, more intimate form of argument. If you can substitute "I think" for "I feel" in a statement and the statement still makes sense, you are expressing a thought not a feeling. Feelings in marriage should not remain unexpressed. It can be a bit of a challenge, however, to surface the feelings gracefully in a context of civility. One couple with a good communications history in their marriage used the simple code expression, "I'm upset," whenever either wanted to open up a conversation about whatever it was that was "bothering" him or her, making either *feel* uneasy or uncomfortable. Spring the code word and you can count on having good acoustics; you can depend on having a respectful, attentive listener. Another way of keeping the potential for blowups to a minimum is to convince your partner that a really supportive spouse is one who has no immediate plans for your improvement.

Arguments will crop up from time to time. It is good to argue by mutual consent. There is no "good" time for the argument, but some times are better than others. Some newlyweds will receive this advice: "Never let the sun set on an argument." In these days of "instant messaging," some prefer to take the I.M. route to raising thorny issues while avoiding eye-to-eye contact. Decide when and how you are going to talk it out, but don't let the elapsed time function as a mechanism to avoid confrontation and resolution. And when you are in an argument, remember that it will go a whole lot better if each of the participants agrees to hear the end of each other's sentences. Remember: the end!

Here for your pondering (and amusement) is a poem by Samuel Hazo:

How Married People Argue
> Because they disagreed on nuclear
>   disarmament, because he's left
>   the grass uncut, because she'd spilled
>   a milkshake on his golf bag,
>   he raced ten miles faster
>   than the limit.

> Stiffening,
>   she scowled for him to stop it.
> His answer was to rev it up
>   to twenty.

> She asked him why
>   a man of his intelligence would
>   take out his ill temper on a car?
> He shouted in the name of Jesus
>   that he never ever lost
>   his damn temper.

She told him
   he was shouting—not to shout—
   that shouting was a sign of no
   intelligence.

He asked a backseat
   witness totally invisible
   to anyone but him, why women
   had to act like this.

She muttered,
   "Men," as if the word were mouthwash
   she was spitting in the sink.

Arriving
   at the party, they postponed the lethal
   language they were saving for the kill
   and played "Happily Married."

Since all the guests were gorging
   on chilled shrimp, the fake went
   unobserved.

She found a stranger's
   jokes so humorous she almost
   choked on her martini.

He demonstrated
   for the hostess how she could
   improve her backswing.

All the way
   home they played "Married
   and so what."

She frowned as if
   the car had a disease.

He steered
   like a trainee, heeding all
   speed limits to the letter,
   whistling "Some Enchanted Evening"
   in the wrong key, and laughing
   in a language only he could
   understand.

At midnight, back
   to back in bed, he touched
   the tightness of her thigh.

She muttered,
   "I'm asleep," as if her permanent address
   were sleep.

He rose and roamed
   the darkened house, slammed
   every door he passed and watched
   a prison film with George Raft.

Abed at dawn, he heard
   the tears she meant for him
   to hear.

He listened and lay still.
Because they both had round-trip
    tickets to the past but only
    one-way tickets to the future,
    he apologized for both of them.

They waited for their lives to happen.
He said the hostess's perfume
    Was Eau de Turpentine.

She said
    the party was a drag—no humor.
Word by word, they wove themselves
    in touch again.

Then silence
    drew them close as a conspiracy
    until what never was
    the issue turned into the nude
    duet that settled everything
    until the next time.

When the wife of former U.S. Senator Harris Wofford
died, her obituary in the *Philadelphia Inquirer* ended with
these words of her husband: "Fifty-two years together, and
each time I would say, 'You're my best friend,' she would
say, 'I'm your sharpest critic.' And each time I would say,
'You're my sharpest critic,' she would say, 'But I'm your best
friend.' And they were both true."

TWENTY-FOUR

Blessing

Whenever I officiate at a wedding, I remind the guests that they, like me, are there as witnesses. As the official witness, my name and signature will be on the marriage license. But all present are unofficial witnesses to the promise, and after the exchange of vows and rings, I usually ask the congregation to express approval of what has just happened in their sight and hearing by giving the couple a warm round of applause.

Later in the ceremony, I ask the congregation to assist me in invoking God's blessing—the special nuptial blessing—on bride and groom by raising their hands as I raise mine over the heads of the newly married couple.

First the celebrant will say to the congregation, "My dear friends, let us turn to the Lord and pray that he will bless with his grace _____ [the bride] now married in Christ to _____ [the groom], and that he will unite in love the couple he has joined in this holy bond." Then come the words of the nuptial blessing:

> *Father, by your power you have made everything out of nothing. In the beginning you created the universe and made humankind in your own likeness. You gave man the constant help of woman so*

*that man and woman should no longer be two,
but one flesh, and you teach us that what you have
united may never be divided.*

*Father, you have made the union of man and
wife so holy a mystery that it symbolizes the marriage of Christ and his Church.*

*Father, by your plan man and woman are
united and married life has been established as the
one blessing that was not forfeited by original sin
or washed away in the flood.* [At this point I invite
the wedding guests to raise their hands in the direc-
tion of the couple.]

*Look with love upon this woman, your daughter,
now joined to her husband in marriage. She asks
your blessing. Give her the grace of love and peace.*

*May she always follow the example of the holy
women whose praises are sung in the scriptures.*

*May her husband put his trust in her and rec-
ognize that she is his equal and the heir with him
to the life of grace. May he always honor her and
love her as Christ loves his bride, the Church.*

*Father, keep them always true to your com-
mandments. Keep them faithful in marriage and
let them be living examples of Christian life.*

*Give them the strength that comes from the
gospel so that they may be witnesses of Christ to
others. Bless them with children and help them to
be good parents. May they live to see their children's children. And, after a happy old age, grant
them fullness of life with the saints in the kingdom
of heaven. We ask this through Christ our Lord.*
[And the congregation gives a resounding] *Amen.*

TWENTY-FIVE

Gratitude

If I were pressed to the wall for a one-word summary of the essential meaning of all religion, I would say, "Gratitude." In my view, that one word says it all. Now, someone might argue that "love" would be a better reply, and I'd concede that a good case could be made for that substitution. But I would stick with "gratitude" and point out that in the First Letter of John we read: "In this is love, not that we [first] loved God but that he loved us and sent his Son to be the atoning sacrifice for our sins." This is a scriptural foundation for an entire theology of grace. God first loved us. All we can be is grateful. His love is completely gratuitous; it cannot be earned. He has loved us first; our only response to that love is gratitude.

In the wedding liturgy for my niece Anita Byron and Colin Warmington at Holy Cross Church in Philadelphia on September 7, 1996, gratitude was highlighted in their selection for a second reading of Colossians 3:12–17, the forgiveness text that we've seen before in this book. After stressing the importance of forgiveness as an expression of love, this Scripture passage continues:

> *And be thankful. Let the word of Christ dwell in you richly; teach and admonish one another in all*

wisdom; and with gratitude in your hearts sing
psalms, hymns, and spiritual songs to God. And
whatever you do, in word or deed, do everything
in the name of the Lord Jesus, giving thanks to
God the Father through him.

We all have a lot to be thankful for at any time; bride
and groom have everything to be thankful for on their wedding day. So I talked about gratitude to Anita and Colin and
the congregation of their families and friends.

Anita is my youngest niece. I always called her "the
most beautiful girl in the world." Sometimes, to her embar-
rassment when she was a child, I did that with the aid of the
melody that put those words to music. Well, there she was—
a woman, a beautiful bride, a believer standing at the altar
of her parish church to ask God's blessing on her marriage
and her future with Colin.

"Dedicate yourselves to thankfulness" was the transla-
tion in the text we read that day. And I asked Colin and Anita
to begin doing that right away—thankfulness for each other,
for their parents, friends, faith, health. Dedication to thankfulness is an excellent way to begin a marriage. I also pointed
out that their wedding was being celebrated in the context of
the Eucharist, and Eucharist is all about thanking God.

"You simply cannot afford to be an ingrate, a per-
son who never says thanks, if you want a happy
marriage," I said. "Indeed you cannot be a happy
person if you are so self-enclosed that you never
thank anyone. Not to thank God—the source of

all you have, and are, and will become—not to
thank God is just plain folly."
  So be back here often and regularly at the altar
for Eucharist—for sacramental thanksgiving,
prayerful thanks-saying, and ritual thanks-doing.

I wondered later if Uncle Bill had sounded a bit too much like a Dutch uncle laying down the law of "Sunday obligation," but I don't think so. There was no need to be concerned about that. I've made the same point many times to many others because of my conviction that gratitude is central to our relationship to God. We simply cannot be anything but grateful. And I've often drawn that line of reflection out to make the following point about moral obligation.

In the early American vernacular, "much obliged" was a commonplace expression that substituted for "thank you." When we say thanks to God, we declare ourselves to be much obliged toward God and one another: obliged to praise and thank God, the source of all we possess; obliged to offer grateful service to and sharing with other humans whom God's providence has put within our reach. Good thoughts for the beginning of any marriage.

TWENTY-SIX

Sacrament

It is more than useful to recall, as the wedding day draws near, that marriage is a sacrament. The word *sacrament* suggests something that "makes holy." It serves to remind that marriage is a sacred reality. The Catholic Church might be called a "sacramental" rather than a "congregational" church. Catholics gather in congregations, of course, to hear the word of God proclaimed and to offer their praise and thanks to God, but the liturgical life of the church centers on seven sacraments, none more central than the Eucharist, but all seven are sacramental encounters with the saving, forgiving, healing, caring Christ.

There is visible, audible, tangible "stuff" (in addition to ritual prayers) associated with the sacraments. Water for baptism; chrism for confirmation; an absolving hand and audible word of forgiveness for the sacrament of reconciliation; bread and wine for Eucharist; oil for the sacrament of the sick; imposition of hands and anointing with chrism for holy orders; and for marriage, the joining of hands and the public expression of a promise. Hand and touch are an important part of the church's sacramental life; in a certain sense, the hands speak the silent language of sacraments. *"Take my hand, and lead me to salvation...."*

Catholics are taught that the sacraments not only are "signs," but they effect (i.e., bring about) what they signify. Through the waters of baptism, God saves; the chrism of confirmation strengthens commitment; the absolving hand signals forgiveness; the consecrated bread and wine nourish the faith of the believer and unite the believer not only with God but with all other believers as well; the anointing with oil restores the sick to health—if God so wills. Or, if restoration of health is not God's plan for this person at this time, the anointing brings spiritual strength and courage to the person who is ill. The imposition of hands on those who present themselves for ordination conveys the gift of the Holy Spirit on the person called to ministry.

The sacrament of marriage unites two persons (as their joined hands signify) together for life. The marriage vows that they pronounce in the hearing of a witnessing priest or deacon and the community of their families and friends, bind them in a sacramental promise. The sacrament makes their union holy and provides spiritual strength to keep them faithful to their promise. And when the marriage is consummated, the union is both ratified and perfected; it is complete.

It is helpful to think of the sacraments as situations, places, or events where we can directly encounter Christ. In a sacrament, we encounter his healing and helping hands, his forgiving voice, his loving gaze, his openhanded generosity;

these are ours under the sacramental signs. Each sacrament, including marriage, has its unique way of making us present to Christ and him to us in our own time. They effect what they signify. This we know by faith; and for all of this we are grateful.

TWENTY-SEVEN

Interfaith

In the Fall 2000 issue of *Spirituality & Health*, I came across the following reflection:

> I have often sat in a pew watching a wedding that was beautiful and "religious," and yet I somehow felt something was missing. Many times I felt left out of a wedding because I didn't understand the rituals taking place, or worse, because it was clear that the bride and groom didn't understand them either. They seemed to be going through the motions of a wedding—saying the words, exchanging the rings—but they were not really aware of the tradition that was being celebrated.
>
> When Jon and I were married, I wanted our guests to feel included no matter what their beliefs. I wanted them to be moved by the miracle of our love for each other and by the miracle of two becoming one. I also wanted them to participate spiritually. When friends began to ask, "Is it going to be a religious ceremony?" I needed something to say. My answer began in the form of a prayer:
>
> *Dear God,*
> *I am not inviting you to my wedding just because I want to follow tradition, perform ritu-*

als, or "be religious." I want you there so that you can bless our union and profoundly change an ordinary ceremony into something extraordinary. As we plan our wedding, make us aware of any ritual or observance we can include to celebrate your presence. But also reveal to us anything that is simply an exercise in religiosity. Lord, I want to get married with you actually there, not just mentioned. Please show us how to do that. Amen.

Those are the words of Martha Williamson, executive producer of *Touched by an Angel,* and author of *Inviting God to Your Wedding* (Harmony Books, 2000). She catches a concern that many couples have, particularly those whose faith commitments differ, but who realize that their respective faith traditions have something unique to bring to the ceremony. Acknowledging and respecting the differences is not just a matter of principled honesty; it is a way of finding new beauty in the timeless truth that unity, if it is to be achieved at all, must always emerge from difference.

Often for Jewish-Christian weddings, I recommend a short reading from the Book of Ruth (1:16–17). The words are spoken woman to woman, the widowed Ruth to her mother-in-law Naomi, who wanted Ruth to feel free, after her young husband—Naomi's son—had died, to get on with her life. But the words work at a wedding; they are more than appropriate to express the permanent commitment of woman to man and man to woman in marriage:

But Ruth said, *"Do not press me to leave you or to turn back from following you! Where you go, I*

*will go; where you lodge, I will lodge; your people
shall be my people, and your God my God. Where
you die, I will die—there will I be buried. May the
LORD do thus and so to me, and more as well, if
even death parts me from you!"*

The Benedictine monk Gregory Norbet put these words
to music under the title "Wherever You Go." Many couples
choose this to be sung at their wedding:

Wherever you go, I shall go.
Wherever you live, so shall I live.
*Your people will be my people, and your God will be
   my God too.*
*Wherever you die, I shall die and there shall I be
   buried beside you.*
*We will be together forever, and our love will be the
   gift of our life.*

The reading from Ruth set the tone for the March 2,
2002, wedding in Holy Trinity Church of Evan Ryan and
Tony Blinken. He, a Jew, had been uneasy about having the
ceremony in a Catholic church not so much for personal religious reasons but because his stepfather, who would be present, was a Holocaust survivor and a leader in the Jewish
community in Paris, France. The reading gave me the opportunity to say that two great faith traditions were present
there under one God—"your God my God"—and the ritu-
als from both traditions would be incorporated into this ceremony.

We had a chuppa, the Jewish wedding cano
bol, as a rabbi once told me, of "a home open on all siu⌣
welcoming everyone." And we had at the end of the ceremony the breaking of the glass.

When I assisted Rabbi Lewis Solomon at the wedding
of Jill Silver and Sam DeCastro in Washington, D.C. on
September 9, 2003, Rabbi Solomon explained to this interfaith couple, "In the Jewish tradition, the breaking of the
glass (wrapped in a white napkin) at a wedding is a symbolic
hope that your love for one another will remain until the
pieces of this glass come together. It is also a reminder that
in the midst of all our rejoicing we should be mindful of all
the pain and suffering that exist elsewhere in the world. Let
us, with this symbol, be mindful of the needless barriers that
people erect between one another, and try to think, with the
breaking of the glass, of breaking down barriers and helping
build a world of respect, unity, and peace."

I witnessed another Jewish-Catholic wedding of two
young friends who took their respective personal faith commitments seriously and whose preference for privacy I'm
respecting here by not mentioning them by name. Each had
deep respect for the beliefs of the other. Religion was important in their lives.

On the Sunday morning of their wedding day, I celebrated mass for both families in the home of the bride, a
Catholic, pointing out, as the quiet home mass proceeded,
the ritual links to Passover and ancient sacrificial rites. In the
afternoon wedding the Liturgy of the Word began with this
selection from the Song of Solomon (8:5–7), chosen by the

groom in the hope of conveying to the non-Jewish guests the centrality of the covenant in his religious experience:

> *Who is that coming up from the wilderness, leaning*
>   *upon her beloved?*
> *Under the apple tree I awakened you;*
> *There your mother was in labor with you;*
>   *there she who bore you was in labor.*
>
> *Set me as a seal upon your heart,*
>   *as a seal upon your arm;*
>   *for love is strong as death,*
>   *passion fierce as the grave.*
> *Its flashes are flashes of fire,*
>   *a raging flame.*
> *Many waters cannot quench love,*
>   *neither can floods drown it.*

And for the responsorial psalm, this couple chose Psalm 139, which was read with participation by the full congregation:

> Leader: *O LORD, you have searched me and known me. You know when I sit down and when I rise up; you discern my thoughts from far away.*
>
> Congregation: *You search out my path and my lying down, and are acquainted with all my ways.*
>
> Leader: *Even before a word is on my tongue, O LORD, you know it completely.*

Congregation: *You hem me in behind and before, and lay your hand upon me.*

Leader: *Such knowledge is too wonderful for me; it is so high that I cannot attain it.*

Congregation: *Where can I go from your spirit? Or where can I flee from your presence?*

Leader: *If I ascend to heaven, you are there; if I make my bed in Sheol, you are there.*

Congregation: *If I take the wings of the morning and settle in the farthest limits of the sea, even there your hand shall lead me, and your right hand shall hold me fast.*

Leader: *If I say, "Surely the darkness shall cover me, and the light around me become night," even the darkness is not dark to you; the night is as bright as the day, for darkness is as light to you.*

Congregation: *For it was you who formed my inward parts; you knit me together in my mother's womb.*

Leader: *I praise you, for I am fearfully and wonderfully made. Wonderful are your works; that I know very well.*

Congregation: *My frame was not hidden from you, when I was being made in secret, intricately woven in the depths of the earth.*

Leader: *Your eyes beheld my unformed substance. In your book were written all the days that were formed for me, when none of them as yet existed.*

Congregation: *How weighty to me are your thoughts, O God! How vast is the sum of them!*

Leader: *I try to count them—they are more than the sand; I come to the end—I am still with you.*

The next reading from Zechariah (8:20–23) contained a memorable and most appropriate line for this interfaith assembly: *"Thus says the LORD of hosts: In those days ten men from nations of every language shall take hold of a Jew, grasping his garment and saying, 'Let us go with you, for we have heard that God is with you.'"*

A New Testament reading is always part of a Catholic ceremony; for this the bride chose the familiar "Beatitudes" from the Sermon on the Mount (Matt 5:3–9). Her desire was to let the non-Christian guests hear what she considered to be the central values of her own Christian tradition:

Blessed are the poor in spirit, for theirs is the kingdom of heaven.
Blessed are those who mourn, for they will be comforted.
Blessed are the meek, for they will inherit the earth.
Blessed are those who hunger and thirst for righteousness, for they will be filled.
Blessed are the merciful, for they will receive mercy.
Blessed are the pure in heart, for they will see God.

Blessed are the peacemakers, for they will be called children of God.

All of this provided rich material for the homily. I invited bride and groom, together with their families and friends, to ponder several of the phrases from the beautiful 139th Psalm, to savor them really in a meditative way. "LORD, you have searched me and known me." "You discern my thoughts from far away." "You are acquainted with all my ways." "You lay your hand upon me." And I suggested that they, like countless believers before them over the centuries, could prayerfully admit: "Such knowledge is too wonderful for me; it is so high that I cannot attain it."

We were confronted with mystery in the readings and indeed in marriage itself. "The hand of God has brought you to this moment," I said; "the hand of God will hold you fast."

Not only is the way God deals with you, the way his hand has guided you, a mystery; the God who has brought you to this moment is himself a mystery. I am suggesting that the marriage you enter into today can indeed become an unfolding of the mysterious God, a disclosure of the Godhead, a revelation of what God is like. Your day-to-day union in the demands and delights of marriage can be a disclosure of what God is like.

Marriage is, first and foremost, a covenant relationship. You commit yourselves today to be faithful to that covenant, faithful to one another. Fidelity is central to the reality of who God is, what God does, and how God relates to the men and women he has called into existence, the men and women upon whom he has laid his guiding and sustaining hand. Your own fidelity in marriage is thus a disclosure of what God is like, of God's fidelity.

God is, of course, love. Love is quite literally the sum and substance of God. It is love that brings you here today. It is love that will sustain you in all your days together down through the years into an unknown future. "Where love is, God is." Where you are—in the delights and demands, the deeds and words of love—there God will be for all to see. Your world can surely benefit from that kind of disclosure, from that kind of revelation. As you work out the mystery of marriage, the mystery of how two can in fact be one, you will be unfolding for yourselves and others something of the mystery of God. It is possible to discover in a marriage of two ordinary persons, extraordinary reflections of divine generosity, creativity, patience, trust, persistence, understanding; it is possible to see in a solid marriage reflections of divine forgiveness. It is possible to find there God's love and God's fidelity. It is possible to see there the face of God—not directly, of course, but radiantly in the lives of two generously committed persons like yourselves.

These are lofty thoughts rooted in reflection on the delights and demands of marriage as both mystery and revelation. And these realities meet in any interfaith couple on their wedding day at an intersection fashioned by the guiding hand of God. In marriage, God draws each out of his or her unique individuality, which will not be lost, into the union of a marriage covenant. Adherents to a monotheistic religion, even if the religious expression of belief differs, can relate to the idea of marriage as a covenant blessed by God, and they can live that covenant in peace and fidelity.

It was in the Hotel Washington where Rabbi Harold White and I officiated together at the June 5, 1988, wedding of two young Georgetown physicians, Colette Magnant and David Milzman. Colette, the Catholic partner in this interfaith marriage, is the daughter of longtime friends of mine; they wanted me to remind all present that what they were witnessing was not simply an interfaith wedding, but the marriage of two people who regarded faith as important in their lives. "Each believes *in* something," I said, "not *against* something." Acknowledging that I spoke to them out of that faith tradition that I shared with Colette, I pointed out that the words they had just heard from the famous "love is patient" text in Paul's First Letter to the Corinthians (chapter 13) display a continuity, not a break, with David's faith tradition. And I indicated that one of the countless places in that tradition where one can find a root for the "love is kind; love is patient" word of the New Testament is in the prophet Micah, where it is written: "He has told you, O mortal, what is good; and what does the LORD require of you but to do justice, and to love kindness, and to walk humbly with your God?" (6:8).

After quoting Micah, I said: "Both of you, Colette and David, believe in God. You believe in the same God. You believe in a God who invited you, in the words of David's tradition, to act justly, to love tenderly, and to walk humbly with your God. And you begin doing that together today as husband and wife."

This, of course, is what makes an interfaith marriage something so profoundly and beautifully different from a structured experience of intercultural cooperation and understanding. It is a gift to be celebrated, a mystery to be pondered.

TWENTY-EIGHT

Money

When Daria Lin and Ed Guelig were married on August 23, 1980, they told the assembly of friends and family a lot about themselves with the Gospel reading they chose for their wedding mass:

> *Therefore I tell you, do not worry about your life, what you will eat or what you will drink, or about your body, what you will wear. Is not life more than food, and the body more than clothing? Look at the birds of the air; they neither sow nor reap nor gather into barns, and yet your heavenly Father feeds them. Are you not of more value than they? And can any of you by worrying add a single hour to your span of life? And why do you worry about clothing? Consider the lilies of the field, how they grow; they neither toil nor spin, yet I tell you, even Solomon in all his glory was not clothed like one of these. But if God so clothes the grass of the field, which is alive today and tomorrow is thrown into the oven, will he not much more clothe you—you of little faith? Therefore do not worry, saying, "What will we eat?" or "What will we drink?" or "What will we wear?" For it is the Gentiles who strive for all these things; and*

> *indeed your heavenly Father knows that you need*
> *all these things. But strive first for the kingdom of*
> *God and his righteousness, and all these things*
> *will be given to you as well. So do not worry*
> *about tomorrow, for tomorrow will bring worries*
> *of its own. Today's trouble is enough for today.*
>
> (Matt 6:25–34)

It didn't occur to me after the ceremony to ask my friend Paul Lin, the father of the bride, whether that reading gave him any concern about the future economic security of the bride he had just "given away." I doubt that it did, however, because he knew these two well and realized that their commitment to simplicity was in fact a commitment to the permanence of the commitment they sealed on that beautiful August day in Rydal, Pennsylvania. That indeed is how their marriage has unfolded over the years.

Paul was far more fortunate than another of my friends whose daughter's wedding I witnessed a decade earlier. I knew that this New Jersey couple planned to live in California after the wedding. When I asked the groom, just by way of small talk about an hour before the ceremony, "What will you be doing out on the West Coast?" he replied: "Getting by, just as I've been doing here." Regrettably, neither the "getting by" financially nor the marriage itself worked out.

"Wedding Joy, with Separate Checking" read the headline over a May 22, 1993 *New York Times* story about newlyweds finding ways to maintain some financial independence. A photo inset to the article, appearing to be a wedding invitation, bore the heading, "Premarital Financial Checklist:

Things to Remember." And here is the list of items to be checked:

- Ownership of checking and savings accounts
- Beneficiaries of retirement accounts and pension plans
- Changing title on marital residence or the names on the lease
- Credit card ownership
- Payment of existing debts
- Who will handle payment of regular bills
- How joint expenses will be paid
- Insurance coverage: life, medical, and property
- The handling of investments
- Personal protection of prior assets
- Support obligations from a prior marriage
- Support obligations for aging parents
- Taxes on the sale of individual residence

The news story reports that the way newlyweds set up their financial arrangements is changing, "a result of the shifting role of women and the erosion of the presumption that marriage is forever." That's enough to get anyone's attention and surely a reason for prayer, discussion, and prenegotiation on the part of those preparing for marriage.

Nothing wrong with the idea of prenegotiation: Whose career follows whose, when geographic relocation will be involved? Do bank accounts merge with the union of minds and hearts when two persons become one flesh in marriage?

Money matters before and throughout any marriage. The six-week marriage preparation program (six successive Thursday evening, two-hour sessions) at Holy Trinity Catholic Church in Washington, D.C., where I served as pastor for three years before moving on in 2003, devoted a full evening to the experience the engaged couples had in their own lives of family traditions and values. In this context, discussion is encouraged about decision-making and money management.

How did your family deal with money? What money "messages" did you receive? Did you think then about how you would deal with money when you grew up? Did money (or its absence) affect your sense of self-worth?

Money is a window into a lot of important considerations surrounding a marriage (not the least of which is the expense of the reception!), but if there is a link between money possessed and a sense of self-worth, there is no more important consideration to be addressed than this by way of freeing up that insecure self for the gift of self in marriage.

An indirect route to this issue, although worthy of direct consideration on its own merits by those who do not need dollar signs to measure self-worth, is the household budgeting consideration. We asked couples preparing for marriage at Holy Trinity to think about this:

Assuming that yours will be a two-paycheck marriage, would you consider gearing your standard of living to just one salary? Not everyone can do

*it, of course, but some have set aside the newly
married wife's earnings (the net after taking out
the expenses associated with going to work, like
wardrobe and transportation) in an escrow fund
for future use in meeting maternity expenses, purchase of home and furniture, and other major out-
lays. Rent, groceries, entertainment, and vacation,
along with other ordinary expenses, will be cov-
ered by the other paycheck. Then, if the new wife
becomes a new mother and chooses not to return
to work, there is no reduction in the family standard of living and no danger (as, sadly, sometimes
happens) of resenting the new arrival as being the
cause of a sharp reduction in the couple's standard
of living.*

"Time, Sex and Money: The First Five Years of
Marriage" is the title of an article in *America* magazine
(May 14, 2001) that is worth reading by those on their way
to the altar. It is coauthored by Michael G. Lawler and Gail
S. Risch, director and researcher, respectively, at Creighton
University's Center for Marriage and Family. They con-
ducted a study of the first five years of marriage and found
that the big three problem areas, the three pressure points on
stability and happiness in the early years of marriage, are (1)
balancing time between job and family, (2) the frequency of
sexual relations, and (3) money matters like the amount of
debt brought into a marriage, the husband's employment,
and the couple's financial situation.

Balancing job and family and the frequency of sexual
relations led the list of issues needing resolution in the early

years; money matters came in third on the chart of forty-two issues examined. The authors open their sobering article with these words:

> *Two of the most troubling aspects of American society today are the high rate of divorce and the fact that divorce in one generation increases the likelihood of divorce in the next. Current divorce statistics indicate that most divorces occur for couples married less than five years and that the proportion of divorces is highest for couples married three years. This is not surprising, since [our] recent study finds that couples face serious conflicts over the use of time, sex and money in their first years of marriage.*

There is no postponing the pondering of these points by those about to enter into marriage. To make that pondering both prayerful and productive, go back to the beginning of this chapter and, wherever possible, substitute "money" for the items Jesus urges you not to worry about! All of us are the target audience for the "O, ye of little faith" message. Just rely on the little faith you have to strengthen your resolve not to let yourself, or your marriage, be possessed by your possessions.

TWENTY-NINE

Anniversary

If "love is what you've been through with someone," wedding anniversaries have a way of tempering idealism (the ideals highlighted throughout this book) with the realism (the day-to-day, year-in-and-year-out, practical, down-to-earth, "being through") of marriage. "Would you do it all over again?" is a question not for the faint of heart; it could ruin the anniversary celebration!

Victor Villaseñor, an American of Mexican descent, tells, in a book titled *Thirteen Senses* (Rayo/HarperCollins), the story of his parents as newlyweds and young parents, and carries the story forward to a moment picked up in the September 9, 2001, review of this book in the *Washington Post* by Ruben Navarette Jr.:

It's the summer of 1979, and Juan Salvador Villaseñor and Maria de Guadalupe Gomez are marking their 50th wedding anniversary by renewing their vows in front of their children, grandchildren and great-grandchildren—all squeezed into the living room of the family home in Oceanside, California. What might have been an uneventful ceremony gets spiced up in a hurry when Lupe, Victor's mother, to her family's horror, hesitates when asked by the priest if she will again take this man to be her wedded husband in good times and bad.

Reflecting on the bad times—especially in the first few years of marriage—leaves Lupe wondering if, knowing then what she knows now, she would have struck the original bargain 50 years earlier.

You can read the book to get the full, rich story of this marriage. I will simply add a bit more from the review to show that realism can indeed temper idealism over the years without at all diluting the rich wine of a fine marriage.

Villaseñor succeeds in showing us everything that the two people meant to one another and to those around them. Along the way, he lays bare the notion of the "thirteen senses"—the complete range of human feeling supposedly experienced by a man and woman when they join in *amor.*

Thirteen Senses is not only a stirring memoir of a single marriage but also a timeless love story. Despite Lupe's doubts, the union proves to have the kind of love that withstands time, overcoming tests and obstacles and tragedies; no one even contemplates throwing in the towel. In the end, we are reminded that, in marriage—as in any relationship—the wrinkles and blemishes are what bring out the beauty.

Mention of Oceanside, California prompts me to recall being there in June 1995 for the wedding of Tom Egler, whose mother Ruth has been a friend of mine since college days, and Margaret Webb. The wedding took place at noon in the mission church of San Luis Rey. Printed on the certificate of completion of their marriage preparation program, sent me a few months earlier by Tom and Margaret, were the words: "A wedding is a day; a marriage is a lifetime." I knew that Tom's parents were approaching their 50th anniversary, so I alluded to that lifetime together while highlighting a phrase this young couple had in their first reading (Song of Songs 8:6–7); it was rendered in these words: "The flash of [love] is a flash of fire, a flame of the Lord himself." And I said:

> *Your love, Tom and Margaret, and your love over these many years, Ruth and Fred, and your love also, Reed and Mary Ann [Margaret's parents], your love for one another is "a flame of the Lord himself."*

Both sets of parents had shown by their good example of love for one another how to keep that flame alive, and by doing so had kept the Lord himself alive in their respective homes for their children.

It was at another wedding—a wedding rehearsal, to be more specific—some years later, that the father of the groom, John Haas, said to me, "I'm going to tell him tonight what my father told me on the eve of my wedding: 'The best thing you can do for your children is to be very good to their mother.'" Good advice generation after generation.

Christmas 2003 brought a letter from Peggy and Holt Williams, of Houston, saying that among their other good experiences in the year just ending, "We also celebrated our

30th wedding anniversary in Mexico where we originally honeymooned and wondered how it could possibly have been thirty years when neither of us felt old enough!" They'll feel the same way when their 50th rolls around.

The famous jurist Benjamin N. Cardozo, when officiating at a wedding in 1931, said:

> *Three great mysteries there are in the lives of mortal beings: the mystery of birth at the beginning; the mystery of death at the end; and, greater than either, the mystery of love. Everything that is most precious in life is a form of love. Art is a form of love, if it is noble; labor is a form of love, if it be worthy; thought is a form of love, if it be inspired.* (cited in John T. Noonan Jr.'s review of *Cardozo* by Andrew L. Kauffman in the *New York Times,* January 21, 1998)

Thinking back on love and marriage from an anniversary perspective can indeed produce inspiring words. But anniversary time also opens the reflective mind to the real struggles any marriage project entails. "Long, happy marriages take work, work, work" was the headline over Jane Brody's "Personal Health" column in the *New York Times* on July 29, 1992. How true, and therefore how satisfying to look back when any anniversary of an intact marriage is celebrated!

Novelist Richard Bausch, who claims that everything he has written is about love, said in an interview with the *Washington Post* (March 2, 1992):

When I go to the movies and they walk off into the happy sunset, I always wonder about three years down the road, with a baby crying and sour stomach....it's like a form of spiritual arthritis—when the person comes down the stairs, I see the inevitable bad outcome. To me love doesn't reside in all those pretty sunsets. Love isn't there, love is in the daily stuff, the way we live our lives. What interests me is all those areas—those irredeemable sorrows we have to deal with.

The *Post*'s interviewer, Elizabeth Kastor, adds: "And the most essential sorrows and joys are locked within the family. The author happily wraps himself in the tangle of family relationships." Anniversaries unlock the sorrows together with the joys and, as most anniversary celebrants will smilingly admit, the joys redeem the sorrows every time.

That's the way it has been for Martie and Bob Gillin, friends of mine since high school days. I've officiated at the weddings of five of their children and assisted at the funeral of one son. Bob and Martie heard a priest say to them on their own wedding day in 1957, the words recalled in the opening chapter of this book, namely, that the future "with its hopes and disappointments, its successes and its failures, its pleasures and its pains, its joys and its sorrows, is hidden from your eyes. You know that these elements are mingled in every life, and are to be expected in your own." All those elements have been part of the Gillin family experience.

So it was with Martie and Bob very clearly in mind that I incorporated into the homily I gave at the wedding in 1999 of their son Steve and Leslie Gilbert, the following words from the song "The Voyage," made famous by the Three Irish Tenors:

Life is an ocean,
   love is a boat;
In troubled waters
   it keeps us afloat.

When we started the voyage,
   there was just me and you.
Now look around us,
   we have our own crew.

Family gives us the security and support we need on our transit through life. What a joy it is to have the crew gather round for those anniversary celebrations that come in the evening of life when the voyage is closer to the end than to the beginning and the marriage is still afloat!

Acknowledgments

My thanks to my Jesuit friend Steve Rowntree, of Loyola University in New Orleans, for reading the manuscript and providing helpful comments. I am grateful to Samuel Hazo, Director of the International Poetry Forum in Pittsburgh, Pennsylvania, not only for permission to include "How Married People Argue" in Chapter 23, but for other suggestions and encouragement as well.

Author

William J. Byron, SJ, is research professor at the Sellinger School of Business, Loyola College in Maryland. During the 2003–4 academic year, he served as interim president of Loyola University in New Orleans. From August 2000 until June 2003, he was pastor of Holy Trinity Catholic Church in Washington, D.C. He taught "Social Responsibilities of Business" from 1992 to 2000 in the McDonough School of Business at Georgetown University, where he held an appointment as Distinguished Professor of the Practice of Ethics and served as rector of the Georgetown Jesuit Community. From 1982 to 1992 he was president of The Catholic University of America. Prior assignments include service as president of the University of Scranton (1975–82), dean of arts and sciences at Loyola University New Orleans (1973–75), and various teaching positions in his field of economics and social ethics.

Father Byron writes a syndicated biweekly column ("Looking Around") for Catholic News Service and a monthly feature "What Would You Like to Know?" for *Catholic Digest*.

Also by William J. Byron, SJ

Quadrangle Considerations (1989)

Take Courage: Psalms of Support and Encouragement
(editor, 1995)

Finding Work without Losing Heart (1995)

Answers from Within (1998)

Jesuit Saturdays (2000)

A Book of Quiet Prayer (2006)*

*available from Paulist Press